This

MANAGERIAL CONSULTING SKILLS
a practical guide

To Charles Murphy
for his consulting advice and tuition

Managerial Consulting Skills
A practical guide

Charles J. Margerison

Gower

Published by
Gower Publishing Company Limited,
Gower House,
Croft Road,
Aldershot
Hants GU11 3HR,
England

Gower Publishing Company,
Old Post Road,
Brookfield,
Vermont 05036,
USA.

British Library Cataloguing in Publication Data
Margerison, Charles J.,
    Managerial consulting skills.
    1. Management consultancy
    I. Title
    658.4'6

ISBN 0 566 02793 3

Printed and bound in Great Britain by
Anchor Brendon Ltd, Tiptree, Essex

Contents

Preface

I have spent a lot of time giving advice both as an internal and as an external consultant adviser. This book summarizes the key points I have observed and learnt on the way.

The consulting and advisory role in organizations is more important today than it has ever been. The speed and complexity of the modern organization demands that people specialize and offer advice based on their knowledge and experience. The modern organization depends as much on its professional advisers as it does on its managers or other staff.

In previous times the nature and form of consultancy advice was more limited. Of course legal and financial advisers have been long established. Today they have extended their practices and services and also been joined by a host of other consultant advisers. These range from safety advisers to insurance consultants, computer advisers, engineering specialists, personnel and training advisers and so on. All consultant advisers, whether external or internal, have to influence others if they are to do their job.

This book is written for all advisers, and for managers when they act as advisers. The focus is on the processes you can introduce to facilitate organizational improvement. This, I believe, is the main task of the managerial consultant adviser. It is often difficult to assess how effective you are, but your clients should be able to do things better and more efficiently after you have worked with them.

Throughout the book numerous examples are given based upon our own personal experiences. I have not given details that would identify the clients concerned, in accordance with the confidentiality involved. The cases are there to illustrate general points. In that context, therefore, I have suggested guidelines and provided exercises that you can use to gain some personal assessment and development.

A number of people have helped me in the production of this book. My secretaries, Anne Dombrovskis, Lorraine Gardiner and particularly Jane Aberle, have ensured that the book was produced in an efficient manner.

My clients, particularly Stewart McFarlane and Barry Smith, provided valuable insights. My colleagues Jim Kable, Geoffrey Prideaux, Bob Dick and Gordon Wills have read the manuscript and provided most useful advice. I also appreciate the support and advice of Dick McCann and Rod Davies, with whom I have worked on a number of consulting assignments. Also thanks to Jane Fielding for her advice and sub-editing, and to Malcolm Stern for his publishing initiative.

I dedicate this book to my wife Colinette, and my family, for managing effectively and resolving issues without my advice while I was away providing consultation to others.

Charles Margerison

Ways you can use the book

The book has been written so that it can be read and used in sections. You can therefore find the areas you wish to concentrate upon and refer to them when required. The chapters are grouped as shown below.

Part I

Purposes and processes

1. Why managerial consulting is important
2. How to identify the main consulting steps
3. Key processes of consulting
4. Time management and contracting

Part II

Personal and interpersonal skills

5. Interpersonal consulting skills
6. How to gain permission and territory
7. How to raise energy levels
8. How to establish forums for sharing and comparing

Part III

Principles, plans and models

9. What is your consulting model?

Part IV

Politics and pressures

Part I deals with the practical steps you can take to establish an effective consulting relationship. It identifies in particular the different steps involved in consulting.

Part II concentrates on the personal and interpersonal aspects of consulting relationships and shows by case example how to deal with specific issues such as conversation control.

Part III describes how you can look at your consulting work in a strategic way through the use of plans, models and systems in the context of the principles you think are important.

Part IV completes the book by examining the important political factors and pressures that have to be positively managed in any assignment. This leads to a summary overview of the factors associated with failure and success in consulting assignments.

Throughout the book various consulting examples have been introduced from other people who have also written about key points from their professional practice.

The book can be used as a text for management programmes on consulting and advisory skills. Various exercises have been developed at the end of each chapter for this purpose. In addition, your own case examples should be introduced when reading and discussing each section to provide learning points.

Throughout the book I have summarized some of the basic ideas of other consultants who have published their work. These consulting examples are indented and set in a different typeface for easy reference and they appear as follows:

Consultants	Chapter
The Tavistock Institute	1
Peter Drucker	2
Rensis Likert	3
Peter Block	4
Edgar Schein	6
Chris Argyris	7

Consultants	Chapter
Gordon Lippitt	9
Reg Revans	10
International Management Centre	10
Tom Peters and Bob Waterman	11
Hal Leavitt	11
Dick Beckhard	13
Carl Rogers	14
B. F. Skinner	14
Victor Frankel	14
Ian Mangham	15
Larry Greiner and Robert Metzger	16

Clearly this does not cover all the individuals and institutions who have made a contribution. I have not included illustrations from the major private consulting organizations, as it is their job to highlight their work.

My selection reflects those people and organizations that have captured my attention and influenced me. Having said that, my own approach has been shaped by the assignments and clients I have met along the way. I have therefore learned from experience.

In this process I learned from many consultant advisers with whom I have worked along the way. Four of them have been of particular significance. Charles Murphy as a tutor gave me structure, support and intellectual guidance at a formative period when we were at the Birkenhead Technical College. Norman Maier showed me new approaches to education and how to use them. Reg Revans has has a great impact on my career with his philosophy and example of how action learning can transform people's performance at work. Finally, Gordon Wills, through his example of educational vision, enthusiasm and determination over twenty years, has been and continues to be a colleague whose advice I value in developing and implementing ideas that make a real improvement in my own and others' managerial performance.

This particular book is a record of the various points I have learned from experience. I hope that you will also keep your own record of experience and in due course publish it in an article or book so we may all learn from each other. I wish you well in your work.

Part I
PURPOSES AND PROCESSES

1 Why managerial consulting is important

'Friendly counsel cuts off many foes'.

William Shakespeare

Successful managers and organizations today are dependent upon top class consultant advisers. This book highlights some of the skills and processes used by people who are effective in professional consultation.

It is therefore valuable to all those who either offer advice or are in the position of receiving it in order to improve organizational and managerial performance. The book is based on practical examples and illustrations of the factors that either aid or hinder managerial consultants in their work.

Benefits to be gained

The main benefits you gain will be in your influencing skills rather than your technical competence. The specific outputs that you will be able to point to will include the following issues.

Your advice will be used more often

It is a common complaint of consultant advisers as well as managers that people do not act on the information that they provide. It is not so much that people reject the advice, as that they very often ignore it.

Very often such advice can be accurate and relevant to the issues under consideration, but still nothing happens. If this is the situation you face, then you have to look carefully at the way in which you are seeking to influence the other person and the situation in which they find themselves. I have therefore focused on some of the strategies of conversational control that you can use in order to be more effective. In order to influence others you need to be able to control your own conversation and wider interpersonal skills as the starting point. There are various

3

ways of doing this and in the process you will find that you will have a higher percentage of successful interventions.

More job satisfaction

Being in a job where you are giving advice to others can be frustrating, particularly if other people do not implement your proposals. You can often work long and hard and then find that most of the effort has been wasted because nothing happens. Improving your skills as a consultant adviser should also improve your job satisfaction insofar as you are able to chart the stages of an assignment and make on-line corrections as you go. Again, the result will be a higher strike rate.

Opportunities for other challenging work

It is very rare that people will put challenging advisory assignments on your desk as a gift. You need to know how to obtain them in a professional way. By building upon the successes that you have, and presenting them in such a way that clients can see your competence, then you will inevitably get more challenging assignments. There are various ways of doing this without being a foot in the door salesperson, and these methods and approaches are outlined.

Developing win/win relationships

It is important in any advisory work to establish a relationship where the client's identity is enhanced. Often people don't like asking for advice because they feel in some way they will be seen to be inadequate. The important thing about establishing a win/win relationship is that the client recognizes that your relationship with them enables them to make a real contribution to the solution of the problem and they gain personally from your intervention.

More productive use of your time

The job of the consultant adviser can be very time-consuming. It involves a considerable amount of time listening to what other people say as well as putting forward proposals. Therefore, if you are to be effective you need to manage your own time as well as that of your clients. Various ways have been developed for looking at how projects should be managed to improve efficiency. One vital aspect of this is to raise the energy of those around you so that everyone is contributing to the advisory assignment, rather than it all being put on your shoulders. The processes for doing this are discussed in detail.

More useful outputs

At the end of the day clients judge our effectiveness on whether the results that they are achieving are better than before our intervention. We therefore need to be clear on what we are trying to achieve and how we can do it. All of this goes beyond technical knowledge and skill, to looking at the specific consulting processes. These are described in detail and guidelines are given on how you can use them.

What do we mean by consulting and advisory work?

While some people, like legal advisers, accountants, and management development professionals, spend most of their life in consulting and advisory work, line managers also spend a good deal of time advising and using consulting skills. For example, managers regularly have to consult with colleagues in other departments to gain information and give advice on how to proceed. They may also be involved in project groups or task forces to come up with recommendations for a committee or board of directors. Equally, managers have to coach and advise their staff on such matters as work performance and careers. Therefore the skills and processes of consultation and advice are widely used.

Ways you can consult

In any consulting assignment there are four roles from which you can operate, as shown in the model.

External consultant

	A External consultant advising client	B External project manager advising clients
	C Internal specialist staff advising colleagues	D Internal manager advising subordinates or colleagues

Adviser ————————————————————— Executive

Internal consultant

The consulting activity can be undertaken from either an advisory or an executive role.

Role A: This is the conventional notion of an external consultant who provides special advice on contract for a time to clients.

Role B: This is a more recent consulting role, developed in the construction and computer industries particularly, where a project manager from an outside organization has responsibility for delivering an assignment but acts as a consultant to the clients and a line manager in his or her own organization.

Role C: Here a full time executive can act as a consultant to his or her colleagues in a coaching and supporting way.

Role D: This is a role which has grown rapidly in most organizations over the last few years. Today there are many internal advisers on various issues such as finance, safety, law, marketing and so on.

The tasks of consultant advisers

The job of consultant advisers is essentially to help improve individual and organizational performance. In doing that they may use very different methods. However, all of them will be involved in finding out what the problems or opportunities are, assessing the options and providing some guidance and information. This may seem a rather simple threefold approach and in some cases it is.

However, when you see the problems and opportunities within the context of the politics of organizational life then the consulting process is a complex one. It involves talking with many different people, at different levels, with different perceptions, in order to grasp the main facts and feelings about the issues. It then involves a careful assessment to see what can be done that will make an improvement. Then comes the difficult job of feeding back the data and helping the clients make an improvement. If it was not difficult they would not employ you in the first place.

As a result of your efforts some change should occur and it should be for the better. Examples are:

- The client learns how to do something new.
- Costs are reduced.
- Productivity goes up.
- Safety improves.
- Quality standards are improved.
- Profit increases.
- Output increases.
- Job satisfaction improves.
- Absenteeism is reduced.
- New products are developed.
- Skill levels are improved.
- Wastage declines.

- Employment increases.
- Rewards improve.
- Sales increase.

This is only a partial list but each item is measurable and important. It is by making such improvements that we can sustain and increase our standard of living. Such improvements enable us to compete efficiently and effectively. The changes that can emerge from sound managerial consultation and advice do make a difference to the way we work and live.

Moreover, we need top class advisers, whether they be internal or external, because that is the only way the busy manager can keep up to date. Peter Drucker has said we live in the information age. To be successful we need the best advice and the best advisers. This book shows how you can both give and receive advice in order to stay ahead and be successful.

Sophocles said 'no enemy is worse than bad advice.' We need to be skilled in understanding our colleagues and clients if we are to help them choose the correct directions and the best means of reaching their destination.

Who are the internal consultants?

Most organizations today employ internal consultants. The accountant is an example, but there is a growing number of other internal consultants. At a meeting with internal consultants from a large oil company I asked the participants to outline their roles. The range of jobs they did was most impressive and I have summarized some of them below.

- Bill was a business development adviser providing information on market opportunities.
- John was an internal auditor looking at efficiency and effectiveness processes.
- Ron was an information systems adviser helping introduce user requirements to production.
- Jean was a training adviser concentrating on technical development skills.
- Elizabeth was an occupational hygiene and safety specialist concerned with improving work practices as well as advising on health issues.
- Alan was a coordinator for the computer information unit helping ensure that the network arrangements were up to date and being used properly.
- Mark was a management development adviser concerned with career planning and management programmes.
- Susan was a public relations adviser ensuring the company magazine was providing information to the media.
- Ian was an industrial relations adviser working to establish a policy throughout the organization on consultation and negotiation.
- Gary was the corporate lawyer advising on contracts.
- Ray was an engineer advising on new work processes and production systems.

These are just a few of the internal consulting roles which now exist. Each one of them has a different technical element to the job, but the consulting elements are very similar. They all have to understand their clients' needs, gain relevant information, provide advice and most of all have the inter-personal and organizational skills to influence change.

Who are the external consultants?

The external consulting role is more established and widely known. In this book I shall concentrate on consulting from my point of view, which in the main has been from an external situation. The emphasis will be on the organization behaviour aspects and interpersonal skill required.

External management consultants have many skills to offer of a technical nature, but they will all need to be good at managing client relationships and organizational behaviour. These skills combined with the technical skills make for a first class consultant.

The technical knowledge and skills will involve external consultants from the following roles being invited into organizations:

- corporate law
- financial planning
- accounting
- marketing
- health and safety
- training and development
- public relations
- scientific research
- engineering planning
- operations management
- recruitment and selection.

This is an incomplete list but it gives an idea of how widespread the managerial consulting role is.

What makes an effective consultant?

We have all had experience as clients and therefore should have a good basis on which to assess a consultant. For example we have all had to receive advice from our doctor. Most of us have taken advice from solici-tors and accountants. I have had work done on houses in which I have lived and therefore taken advice from architects. Whenever we go on holiday we may seek advice from a travel agent. All of this is over and above the advice we gain each day from friends and colleagues.

Therefore we tend to know what we like and dislike in consultants. When teaching a consulting skills course, I asked the participants what they rated as important. The following is a representative list to which you may wish to add your own points.

Effective consultant	*Ineffective consultant*
Listens to understand	Appears superior in attitude
Accepts data without contradicting what client says	Decries what client says as being unimportant
Initially non judgemental	Criticizes or blames client
Concentrates on the assignment as a priority	Has many 'irons in the fire' at your expense
Takes time to assess problems	Shows impatience
Gets to know the problem or opportunity	Proposes instant pre-packed solutions
Summarizes accurately what clients say	Interested in own views, not clients'
Gives confidence through gesture and behaviour	Lacking confidence
Fulfils promises	Fails to deliver
Adopts positive approach	Only points out what is wrong
Works to facilitate action improvement	Works but no positive change emerges

I am always surprised at the consistency and consensus amongst the replies. This I believe signifies that a cultural standard exists for acceptable and unacceptable consultant adviser behaviour.

Clearly consultant advisers need to be knowledgeable in their field but still put the client first. That is, their expertise should support client needs, not dominate them. Over recent years the medical profession has been seeking to learn this. It is often referred to as 'having the right bedside manner'. Patients clearly want their doctor to be a top expert but primarily they want him or her to treat them as people. In the past, too many doctors have been accused of being poor advisers, not because they were technically at fault but because they turned off the clients by their behaviours.

Therefore there are two essential elements in consulting. One is technical knowledge and the other is interpersonal skills. These I shall refer to as content and process. As a consultant you may or may not need technical ability in the area of your client's business. For example, I act as a facilitator to chemical companies, banks, airlines, electricity authorities and other organizations. They require that I have interpersonal and process skills but not necessarily that I make a technical contribution. If you can do both you are a 'specialist'.

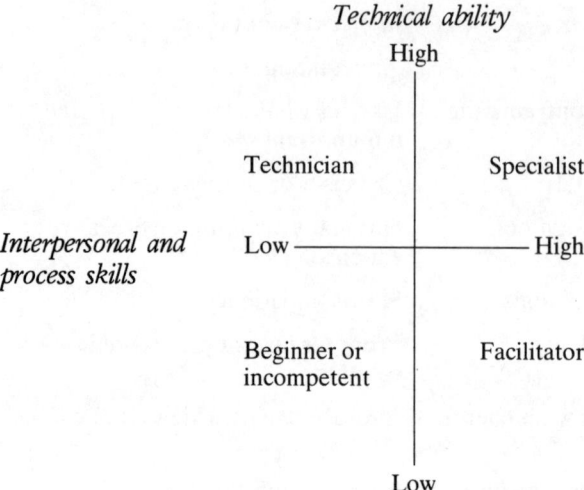

Technical ability

High

Technician | Specialist

Interpersonal and process skills   Low —————————— High

Beginner or incompetent | Facilitator

Low

Two aspects of consulting – people and techniques

Remember most successful consulting involves the management of relationships. Over and above your technical skills people assess you and the way you behave. Either they find you easy to work with or they will look for some way of resolving the problem or opportunity without you.

So look for the points that switch your client on or off. You can often tell by their body language. They will lean forward or backward, they will smile or frown, they will open their hands or close their fists. All are signs and signals. If you can pick up these signals and also relate them to the verbal cues and clues, then you will have one of the most powerful managerial measures within your grasp. To know when people are reacting positively or negatively and how to cope with it is an important consulting skill. The principles outlined in this book provide guidance on how to cope in the challenging role of a management consultant.

Increasingly the modern organization demands that we become more effective in influencing others. The days when a person's position could ensure that they had authority to command others are disappearing. Today organizations are based more and more on professional expertise where people of equal standing in different professions and vocations need to work together. In this sense we all have to consult each other. The hierarchy is being superseded by a laterarchy of interdependent relationships.

The marketing professionals have to gain advice from and give advice to other colleagues. So it is with engineering, production and personnel. We are all involved in consultation as either a client or a consultant. We need to develop consulting skills as an integral aspect of managing.

Putting knowledge into action

The traditional concept of the consultant has been the person of 'knowledge', with the manager the 'executive' who made decisions and took action. Today these distinctions are beginning to change. The consultant, particularly the internal consultant, has to influence people to gain action. Equally the manager has to consult and counsel.

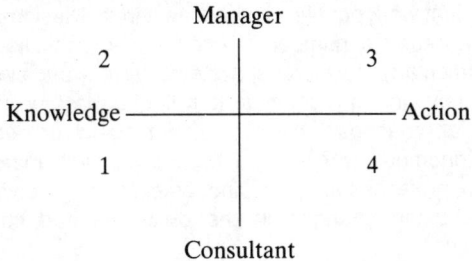

The model above shows the roles that have to be adopted. Often a manager will call upon a consultant to operate in role 1, as information provider, because he or she has encountered obstacles in area 3. The consultant may help the manager become more effective in area 2 before getting back into the action phase.

Consultants have to learn to manage and managers have to learn to consult. Both therefore need to be able to gather knowledge and turn it into effective action. The important thing is that they work in complementary roles and the consultant should learn when and how to influence without taking over the manager's executive accountability.

This is particularly difficult for the internal consultant. It is no use just citing knowledge of the law in safety to production managers. The consultant must bring people together to discuss what the problems are and what can be done to uphold and develop regulations. This needs to be done in conjunction with the managers, who ultimately must see decisions made and carried out. In this sense the consultants are in a joint venture. The name of the game is improved action.

This will mean internal and external consultants must be involved with the day to day politics of an organization and build influence networks to get things done.

P before T and S

Organizations depend on people being able to use technical systems to improve organizational performance. For a long time, however, we have asked people (P) to adapt their behaviour to the new technical (T) and structural (S) systems of production. Examples include the way organizations are structured to minimize peoples' contribution, whether it be repetitive work on the assembly line or lack of structures for consultation.

However, research work initiated by the Tavistock Institute in London many years ago indicated the need to design new technology so that people could relate sensibly. One of the earliest efforts to confront the engineering approach to organizational design were made at the Glacier Metal Company in London. There Eliot Jacques (1951) was employed as an external consultant and worked with the managing director, Wilfred Brown, to find ways of involving staff at all levels in the decision making processes.

Eric Trist (1963) and his colleagues developed another approach based on the concept of the socio-economic-technical system, which encourages job design to reflect work people's involvement in the designs from the early stages. This has seen a number of changes by consultant advisers, in engineering particularly, to various systems from work study through to technological innovation in production to reflect behaviour as well as technology. Modern approaches to this are evident in such processes as quality circles and autonomous working groups. As a result, more emphasis is placed today in professional consulting practice on involving the people whose work is being changed in the diagnosis and consideration of improvements.

Guidelines

The word 'consultation' has always implied giving advice. Its traditional connotation has also implied some people having special knowledge which, when required, can be dispensed at a cost to others.

Today the concept of consultation and consultancy is changing rapidly. It is a set of activities designed to improve things. This can be and is done by managers as well as consultants. The role of consultancy is now multi-faceted. It involves relationships between manager and subordinate just as much as it involves relationships between clients and consultants.

In all these relationships, however, there is a set of governing factors that can help improve performance. This book sets these out based on hard experience together with cases and examples. Although most of the case examples will reflect my role as an external consultant the principles and models are of specific relevance to everyone involved in internal consulting also.

Exercise

1   How would you assess yourself as a consultant adviser? Under the following headings summarize the strengths and weaknesses you bring to consulting and advisory work.

How I see myself as a consultant

Main strengths   Main weaknesses

As a result of this analysis what can you do

   (a) to improve your strengths?

   (b) to reduce your weak areas and improve your performance?

2   What is the most challenging consulting assignment you have had?

3   What are the main things you have learned from consulting activities?

2 How to identify the main consulting steps

Alice: 'Would you tell me, please, which way I ought to go from here?'
Cheshire Cat: 'That depends a good deal on where you want to get to.'

Lewis Carroll, *Alice in Wonderland*

Consulting assignments go through various steps and stages. It is important to know what these are so you can ascertain what needs to be done, when and how. This chapter outlines the steps and stages that I see occurring in most of my work, and illustrates them with reference to an actual consultancy case.

A senior manager in the airline industry, accountable for the performance standards of highly qualified technical staff, met me at a dinner party. He said he had just come back from overseas where he had been looking at new ways of developing the six hundred aircrew who had responsibilities for managing high technology assets and people. He was particularly concerned to improve their teamwork.

I asked him how he felt about the programmes he had seen. 'They are very good,' he said. At this point there was no sign that a consulting problem or opportunity was present. I asked him, 'Are you considering using any of the programmes?' At this point he gave a distinct clue that he was open to discussion on the matter. He said, 'I would like to but I don't think the particular methods they use would be appropriate to our kind of people.'

I enquired what he meant by that. He felt his people would not accept pre-packaged solutions. We began to discuss the possibility of developing an alternative approach. We had begun the consulting process. We had recognized both a problem and an opportunity. I suggested that it might be helpful if I wrote down some ideas for discussion at a later date. He agreed. This case can be used to look at the steps that we went through, as they are involved in most consultancy advisory processes.

The twelve steps in consulting

The following twelve steps provide a basis for assessing any advisory project. Although they are written in a sequential order, real life consulting projects do not always fall easily into such a pattern. You may, for example, still be involved in negotiation yet decide to start gathering data. You may also feed back some of the data before you have finished the data collecting stage.

The 12 steps can be subsumed under the three stages, all As of:

- Appraisal
- Assessment
- Application.

For the purpose of studying what we do, and identifying at any point in time where we are, the following guidelines can be useful:

The four appraisal steps

1 *Contact:* This is the initial meeting to discuss the problem or opportunity. You are approached, or you make the contact, and discuss a broad overview of the issues with an agreement usually to meet again, if you pick up the main cues and the client recognizes your willingness and ability to help.

2 *Preparation:* This is the thinking and preparation time when you may send your initial thoughts to the client and, if they agree, you have meetings for in-depth discussion of the presenting symptoms. It is here that you begin to get to know the actors and their scripts.

3 *Contracting:* This is an outline proposal of what could be done, by whom, when, where, how, why and at what cost. The details are usually written down and sent as a proposal letter after the contracting discussion.

4 *Contract negotiation:* This is where you negotiate the details of a contract. The client assesses the proposal and discusses it with the relevant people before agreeing or proposing amendments prior to agreeing the terms.

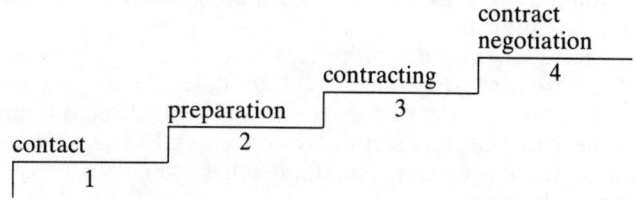

The four assessment steps

5 *Data collection* Assuming a contract is agreed, you proceed to gather relevant data by interviews, group meetings, questionnaires, or whatever is the appropriate approach.

6   *Data analysis and diagnosis:* This is an opportunity to assess the data and review how it should be used with the client, and the set-up of the organizational and meeting arrangements.
7   *Data feedback:* The presentation of the data either orally or by written report or a combination thereof then takes place.
8   *Data discussion:* There follows the discussion of the issues in terms of the objectives and purpose. This is usually best done with the consultant present to clarify points arising and avoid misunderstanding.

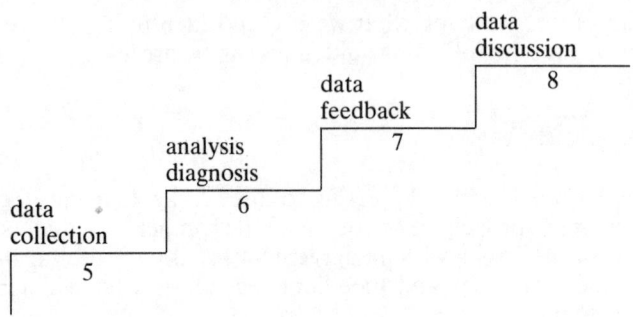

The four application steps

9   *Proposals:* The data feedback at step 7 may or may not have contained proposals. However, proposals will or at least should emerge from the discussion of the data. If possible it is usually best to discuss the data and clarify its meaning separately from discussing proposals for action. The proposal stage is a vital one and should involve considerable concentration on options and opportunities using every creative idea available.
10   *Executive decisions:* The client, individually or collectively, comes to decisions based on the data discussion with or without any advice from you. Ultimately it must be their decision, otherwise you will end up managing their business.
11   *Implementation of the decision:* This is an executive function which from time to time they may want to delegate to you or others. However, a vital aspect of consulting is giving advice on implementation, otherwise the early steps may be wasted. Beware of crossing the thin line between proposing and doing unless you have, by agreement, taken on the latter role.
12   *Review:* An assessment of how the assignment has gone both objectively, in terms of factual results, as well as subjectively, in terms of people's feelings, should take place in order to learn from the intervention.

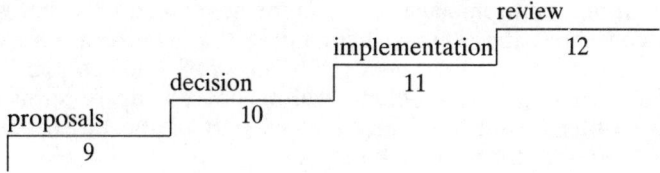

An analysis of the case

Let us assess these steps in the context of the dinner party meeting I had with the Senior Manager. After the dinner party discussion, I went home and made some notes. I was clearly at stage 2, where I could consider and prepare.

Preparation

It was necessary to gather some more information, but before I could do that I had to put forward a basis for taking the matter further. I reflected on what I knew from our initial discussion. These were the essential points:

(a) The senior manager had decided he wanted a programme for his 600 aircrew.
(b) The programme was to last three days.
(c) The budget had been set and the aim was to start within nine months.
(d) He had considered importing an 'off the shelf' solution and rejected it because of the cultural problems of transfer.
(e) Therefore an understanding of the attitudes of his staff and their culture was critical to success.
(f) There were a number of other senior managers who needed to be convinced.
(g) Technical staff could be made available to help with design work.

These were all important items but they certainly did not provide a basis for putting forward a detailed proposal, let alone a solution. We needed a letter which would be an indication of interest which could be circulated to those concerned.

The letter needed to address the issues more by way of reviewing and summarizing the current position and extending an invitation to go further. I therefore summed up these points and indicated the way in which we could work with their organization.

Contracting

The initial letter at this point may be rather general, but at this stage you do not need or want to be too specific. The aim is to find out more, and to establish stronger bonds of communication.

Who will the senior manager bring to the next meeting? What will he or she tell you about the politics surrounding the venture in terms of who needs to be convinced? Who needs to be on side? What content issue will be raised? What specific problems will be brought up in terms of time, money or other resources? These are all part of the initial contracting discussions prior to formal negotiations.

Such meetings are often best set up so you can have two or three 'bites at the cherry'. For example, seek to have the meeting start at about 11.00 am or 11.30 am with an understanding that you will take lunch together. This enables you to have three meetings as follows:

(a)   the pre-lunch formal meeting in an office;
(b)   the informal lunch meeting when others may be brought into the discussion;
(c)   the after-lunch meeting back in the office.

In this way you can get time to think and assess the situation in more depth. You may conclude that you need to spend more time at this stage, which is a vital part of your assessment, before moving on.

Negotiations

Once the contracting discussions have been held, then the draft contract needs to be prepared. It is usually best sent as a discussion document. Such a discussion paper is the prelude to negotiating the contract and getting a written agreement of who is going to do what for whom, when, and for how much and by what time. Such contracts are often created by an exchange of letters, but clearly where there are large sums of money at stake and/or considerable risks involved then it is wiser to have a formal contract even though it takes longer. If you are an internal consultant it is nevertheless important to establish the contract in writing, although it is more likely to be as an exchange of letters.

This will usually be a detailed discussion looking at the costs and time allocation. You need to be careful to estimate your time. Many projects can be open-ended and require a budget that reflects a realistic plan. Be clear on what you are committing yourself to do. Only promise what you feel you can deliver. Cost the project carefully on time, money and resources. Once this has been done and agreed then the consulting assignment can go into full swing.

Data collection

Step 5 is to gather data from those who will be affected by the changes proposed in contrast to those who set up the contract. Your skill in establishing who these people are and getting them together is very important. A former colleague once gave me a phrase which has stuck with me as an important principle in all my work.

'Selection implies rejection,' he said. This is right. Make sure you don't offend people by ignoring their opinion. I always ask my clients, 'Who have we not yet contacted? Who will be affected by this project?' I may reinforce this from time to time in other ways such as 'Who could make it difficult for this project to succeed unless they are asked for their opinion and to participate?'

When gathering data draw a network of all those who for political reasons as well as content reasons need to be involved. Then arrange to gather their views. Use as many ways as are necessary to involve people, from questionnaires to personal interviews.

In between use letters, telephones, facsimile, telex, video, group discussions and so on to gather data.

Data analysis and diagnosis

This usually takes some considerable time. Sifting through data can be a complex job. My own approach is to try and establish a number of areas into which the data falls, then I take what people say and record it verbatim or near verbatim. In short, I let the data 'speak for itself' within broad categories. This is what I did on the airline case and summarized the opinions of the aircrew in their own words as a basis for feedback.

Data feedback

The feedback of the data at step 7 is therefore crucial. It is here your personal skills are particularly important. It is usually of little use just giving a client a report. The important thing is to facilitate a discussion of the data. Therefore consider the best way to feed back the data. Should you circulate the report in advance, then hold a meeting? Should you do both and have people read the report while you personally guide them through it? Each project may require different methods and your skill lies in deciding which is the most appropriate.

There are no golden rules. You need to assess how a client will react. In one of my earliest assignments I wrote a report for a small company in the clothing industry about team organization and sent it to them. A couple of weeks later the chairman of the company asked to see me. He started by saying 'It's a very long report. What exactly does it mean?' Clearly I had used the wrong method with him.

I have used many methods. I tend now to favour working 'arm in arm' with the clients personally so that we gather and assess data as we go along.

Data discussion

The data discussion step is the key to further progress. You must ensure if possible that the politically important people are there. Not only does selection imply rejection but absence will mean lack of understanding. Also ensure you have enough time to discuss the issues. If it is a complex problem, the quick half hour meeting will not be sufficient. Try to get 'three bites of the cherry' by arranging the meetings so they have a lunch or a dinner in the middle to allow consideration in a less formal environment.

Proposals

Try to have a thorough clarification and understanding of the data, however, before going into proposals. It is often best to separate the summary analysis and the proposing stages. Your skill in proposing should be more heavily orientated to the process of how it is done rather than the content. Although you may make proposals in your feedback, the discussions with clients when you consider what can be done are critical.

Don't get locked in too heavily on your own proposal. Put it forward as an option. Ask for other proposals from the clients once they see the data. Listen to their ideas. Often the best proposals are a mixture of their ideas and yours.

Executive decisions

The decisions on the information you provide may take some time. Remember it must the client's decision. They have to live with the consequences. You can advise but they must decide. The doctor or the dentist can suggest it would be best if you had an operation but you, the patient, must make the choice. So it is with business clients. You can point out the options, the consequences, the costs and the benefits, but they must decide.

Implementation

Once the decision is made then the implementation step can begin. The client may or may not want you involved at this stage. If they have the data then they may feel able to get on with the job in their own way. You may not agree but should respect their view. For example, in the airline case the senior manager felt that once we had investigated the requirement and designed a programme we should train his technical staff and let them get on with the job. This is what we did despite initial reservations I had about the strategy. The client's decision was vindicated, as the pilots developed considerable skills as tutors.

Reviewing performance

In order to ensure that progress is as planned, try to build in a review stage. This may be just a half-day meeting three months after implementation or a regular retainer agreement over three to five years. It is important to establish the principle of a review and to carry it out, otherwise much of the early work can go astray. We did this in the airline and regular reviews now take place and improvements are made.

These then are the main steps in consulting advisory assignments. Each one involves different but related skills. I have drawn on a personal case illustration wherever possible to show the issues and dilemmas that arise. In order to provide a framework for you to apply them to your job a number of guidelines and personal exercises are provided so you can assess yourself.

Consulting is a challenging job. There are rarely easy problems or easy answers. Each assignment needs to be looked at in a creative way and I hope the principles outlined enable you to further develop your skills in the important task of consulting.

Strategic consulting for effectiveness

'My greatest strength as a consultant is to be ignorant and ask a few questions.' Peter Drucker

Peter Drucker (1982) is without doubt the best known individual management consultant. His written work is a model of clarity and sound advice in itself. However, he has written relatively little on his own consulting skills although much can be inferred from his work. One of the most straightforward is his small book *The Effective Executive* (1967), first published twenty years ago but still fresh today.

That book provides solid guidelines to us in consulting. Effectiveness can be learned – it is a skill acquired with regular practice providing you practise the right things. Drucker points to the following:

1 Effective people manage their time toward important targets. They allocate priorities and keep to them, for time is their scarcest resource.
2 Effective people focus on outputs and results to be achieved and chart a path to those targets.
3 Effective people build on strengths of themselves and others about them. They do not spend time bemoaning weaknesses. They choose areas they can act upon and concentrate their energies.
4 Effective people make effective decisions based on a systematic approach. They gather the data, work out the options and commit themselves.
5 Effective people develop effective systems. They can reproduce their effectiveness by the use of techniques and methods that improve their productivity and efficiency.

Throughout all his work, Drucker has kept a close eye on what is necessary for success, and has been able to explain the rationale behind the action. That is what an effective consultant must do for himself or herself and their clients. It is not enough to do a job well. You must be able to understand why and pass on that learning to others.

Drucker has some fine sayings to help us on our way such as

- 'If a person wants to be considered responsible for what he/she does, then they have to concern themself with the usability of their product, that is their knowledge.'
- 'The four basic requirements of effective human relations – communications, teamwork, self development and the development of others.'
- 'Knowledge workers don't produce a thing. They produce ideas, information, concepts. Therefore he or she must concentrate on who will use these as outputs and work with them to that end.'
- 'I'm not a bit concerned who is right. That's why I don't belong in academia.'

Peter Drucker is concerned with what works. He has concentrated on a strategic approach to consulting linked to an organizational design and structure focus. He has concentrated on his strengths, as he notes in his autobiography, *The Adventures of a Bystander* (1982). This and his other works are of value in providing a wide business and environmental map within which we can understand our own approach to consulting.

Guidelines

All consulting assignments have steps and stages. It is important to define them, not only to know where you are and what you are doing but to ensure your client also knows what to expect. The twelve steps outlined here can be broken down into three stages.

Initially there is the stage of *appraisal*. This covers all the steps up to number 4, where the formal writing of a contract takes place. It therefore includes negotiation. Appraisal involves the initial contact, preparation and contracting. Interpersonal skills are crucial at these stages in order to get the job.

The next stage is *assessment* of problems and opportunities, in which data is gathered and analysed. This stage, from steps 5 to 8, also involves many interpersonal skills, particularly where it is necessary to gather people's views face to face. It covers the main steps of data gathering through to feedback and discussion and can take a lot of time, particularly in analysing the data.

The final stage is *application*. This covers steps 9 to 12. It includes the formulation of an action plan, the taking of a decision and its implementation and review. This stage is concerned with working out what can be done to improve things and the practical method of how it should be done.

You may feel your strengths in consulting differ according to the phase and stage of the assignment. Review the recent assignments you have had and pick out the steps and stages at which you could have improved your performance. By doing this and breaking the assignment into stages you can then start to prepare a plan for improvement.

Exercise

1   Of the stages and phases listed above, which are the ones that:
    (a) create the most difficulty for you?

    (b) you feel are the easiest to do?

2   What are your personal development plans for improving specific con-
    sulting advisory skills?

3   Consider one of the major projects in which you have been involved
    and record the action you have taken at the various stages.

    *Project title*_____

    (a) *Initial contact*. How was it acquired?

    (b) *Preparation*. What did you do?

    (c) *Contracting*. What was proposed?

    (d) *Negotiation*. What was agreed?

(e) *Data collection.* What information did you collect?

(f) *Data analysis.* How did you analyse the data?

(g) *Data feedback.* How did you feed back the data?

(h) *Data discussion.* What did you do to facilitate data discussion?

(i) *Proposing.* How did you aid with the development of proposals?

(j) *Executive decision.* What was the decision?

(k) *Implementation.* What was done?

(l) *Review.* What was the result?

3 Key processes of consultation

'Experience is the name everyone gives to their mistakes'

Oscar Wilde, *Lady Windermere's Fan*

How we work with others is a crucial factor. In consulting it is probably the most important single thing that determines success or failure. You can be technically knowledgeable, very experienced, and able to do the job, but if you cannot establish the appropriate relationships with the client, then you are unlikely to succeed.

This chapter outlines some of the elements governing the relationship between your clients and yourself. It looks at three main processes of consulting, all of which have to be managed. We shall then look at two different consulting approaches and you can assess which one suits you.

The three action areas

In any assignment you will need to consider three main areas of activity. These all involve action of one kind or the other. The model shows these areas.

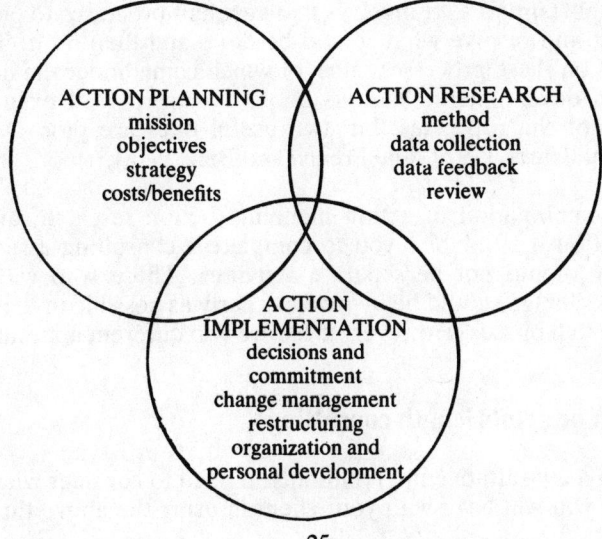

Action planning

In any assignment an important first step is to establish the mission, the goals and objectives. As a consequence, you can begin to set out a schedule of activities which indicates what should be done, by whom and when. This will not be a final plan, but one that develops as you proceed.

Action research

The second area is that of action research. This is the process of finding out what is required. It will involve various methods such as developing a set of questions that need answering and establishing whether to use interviews, questionnaires or other means to gather the data. A founding father of action research was Kurt Lewin (1963). He introduced the method of getting people together in groups for discussion on a subject of importance and writing down their views and comments. A modern exponent of action research is Chris Argyris (1971, 1986). He tape records live business meetings as a means of gaining accurate, valid and reliable data which he can then feed back to his clients. Action research therefore means gathering data from participants as far as possible in a real situation. Then you feed back their data so they can reach conclusions and decide what action should be taken.

Action implementation

All of this leads to the third key area, that of action implementation. It is no use having excellent plans and a great deal of valid and reliable information if no action is taken on them. In that sense action implementation is the most important area. It involves management processes to ensure that people meet and resolve what should be done and then do it. There are many books on these processes, most of which come under the heading of organization development. Various books have provided examples and illustrations of the processes, but two useful ones are those written by Beckhard and Harris (1977) and French and Bell (1978).

It is the combination of action planning, action research, and action implementation that enables you to complete a consulting assignment. I believe they should not be separate activities. Those who will have to implement a change should be involved as early as possible in the planning and the research phases. However, there are two different approaches.

Arm in arm or arm's length consulting

In designing a consultative intervention you need to consider what kind of relationship you will have with your client in using the above three areas.

There are two broad kinds of involvement, which I call arm in arm or arm's length relationships.

Arm's length consulting

The arm's length relationship is characteristic of what I call 'old style' consulting. Here the consultant obtained a brief from a client, then proceeded to work on the assignment without the client having to give much time to it. In essence the consultant would say, 'Leave this with me and I will come up with the answer.'

The client was not concerned about the methods the consultant used. The client's emphasis was on results. This is analogous to the kind of relationship I have with technical people like electricians whom I ask to do work for me. I tell them what needs fixing, and I am not involved with their processes and methods unless they upset my home and way of living. I am concerned only that at the end of the assignment the lights go on, the television works and I can have a cooked meal.

The equivalent of that in managerial consultation is when a client asks for a review of an area and then lets the consultant get on with it. The result is usually that a report is produced a few weeks later. In the intervening time the client and consultant may meet, but only discuss the content of the assignment, not the process. The final report is what counts. Such assignments are based on the assumption of a rational, fact-based, technical approach to consulting.

An example of arm's length consulting is shown in the following case.

A company wanted to know why there was a high level of absenteeism amongst its factory workers and why there was a high turnover amongst the supervisors. A consultant was employed, who sent a questionnaire to all employees. The response rate was 40 per cent. The consultant did a statistical analysis of the responses, wrote a report and submitted it to the client for discussion.

During the assignment the consultant had a few personal interviews with supervisors and operatives, but did not provide any feedback to them or the client at that time. All the data was contained in the report, including recommendations. The board of directors considered the report and decided to hold a course for supervisors and improve working conditions. The supervisors and employees did not see the report.

In this case there was little overlap between the planning, research and implementation or between those involved. The management worked out a plan, consultants did the research and supervisors had to implement the decisions.

Arm in arm consulting

The alternative model is what I term 'arm in arm' consultation.

Here the client indicates the brief as far as possible. The consultant establishes a relationship which can be best summarized as 'let us work on this together'. This signals a relationship where the process of doing the assignment will be as important as the content.

During an 'arm in arm' consultation, the client and consultant will work together to identify the issues, the methods, the data, the analysis and the action required. There may never be a final report, if there is, it could be difficult to tell who contributed what.

It is not that the client and consultant are continually working in each other's offices. They do however keep close contact on developments through telephone calls, the exchange of notes and regular meetings. Their approach is more a joint problem solving endeavour.

In this, they may establish a workshop to carry out the action planning aspects so they become clear on the mission and goals and involve other key players. The consultant would play a leading role in developing a design for the workshop and the way it is conducted, but throughout there would be joint involvement.

Likewise, at the action research stage, it is most likely that the client will be involved in gathering data as well as the consultant, and they will do joint analysis. When it comes to action implementation, it is more likely that the client takes on the leading role and the consultant a counselling role.

'Arm in arm' counselling involves a relationship of considerable trust and confidence. It also involves a situation where both client and consultant are learning from each other. The consultant needs considerable process skills to relate to the political situations and interpersonal skills to cope with the ambiguities of the situation. It is my view that there is a need for more arm in arm consultation as assignments grow more complex.

An example of the arm in arm approach is shown in the following case.

A group of architects were concerned about the development and selection of new partners. They asked me to advise them on how the problem should be tackled. I proposed a series of workshops where all the senior partners attended.

At these regular workshops the senior partners discussed with me the objectives, plans, processes and methods for development and selection. A visual aid was always available for people to write down their ideas so everyone could see them.

An *esprit de corps* emerged amongst the senior partners as they not only worked out a plan, but also gathered the data and worked out how to implement the scheme. Throughout the meetings I helped guide discussions, put in ideas and advised on the processes. The assignment came to a successful conclusion when the partners met their colleagues and worked with them on the development and selection issues to ensure the continuation of the professional practice.

In this case there was a close integration of planning research and implementation by the client group.

What do clients want?

In all assignments it is important to know where you should concentrate. You need to move from one area to another as the situation evolves. The following model shows some of the options.

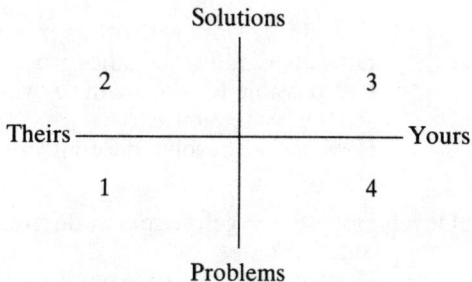

While no approach is always correct, you will do well to start in quadrant 1 on most occasions by asking about the client's problems and opportunities. Then move to quadrant 2 and see if they have any solutions. Often they do, but they have not been tried or tested properly. Where there are no client solutions you can, if it is appropriate, put forward your ideas for discussion. You may of course find that in the assignment the client brings forward issues which involve difficulties for you and it is then appropriate to move to quadrant 4. Knowing where you are will help you advise more sensibly.

Levels of consultation

In any assignment you can be asked to work at different levels. You will be asked to give both personal and technical advice even though you were employed for the latter. Don't be surprised. It is normal and indeed a compliment when someone asks for your advice on personal issues. It means they trust you.

Here are the levels of consultation you may be involved in with some examples of the issues arising.

The individual level	What are my strengths and weaknesses? What training do I need? How can I get to know myself better?
The role level	What career opportunities do I have? How can I manage more effectively? What is my role?

The group level	How can our team improve?
	What is the best balance of work allocation?
	How can we select more suitable people?
	What direction should the team take?
	How do we improve decision making?
	What is our role?

The inter-group level	How do we work with other groups?
	How do we influence other groups?
	Is it possible for our team to 'win' and if so what are the consequences?
	How can we resolve differences of view between groups?

The organizational level	How do we get people in different units to work together?
	How do we set a corporate strategy and plan based on current knowledge?
	How can we design an equitable reward system?
	What should we do with our organization structure to meet the problems we face?

Key actors in the consulting process

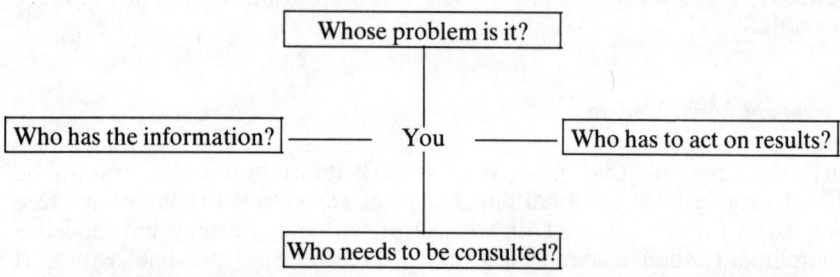

This map can be extremely helpful in clarifying who you should talk to during a consulting assignment. You should draw up a list under each heading of the people you need to meet and what you need to discuss.

Who has the problem?

Whoever has accountability for the resolution of the issue is the person or persons you must meet. He, she or they are your client(s). Make sure they not only brief you but agree with whatever you write down. Moreover keep in close touch with them as you proceed so they can give you advice or further contract instruction. Remember the old saying, 'Keep close to the customer.'

Who has the information?

These people may be in various parts of the organization. Take time to find out by asking around. You will usually find that the people with the information rarely, if ever, meet together. One of the things you can do is bring them together. This in itself often goes a long way toward solving the problem.

Who needs to be consulted?

These people may not have any special information to provide, but they are politically influential. It is vital you keep them in the picture. Let them know what you are doing and how you are going. In that way they can say they have been consulted throughout the process and they may put in a good word at the time when it counts.

Who has to act on the results?

If you are to be successful then those who are critical to implementation need to be identified early. Involve them as soon as possible by getting their views on the difficulties, if any, they foresee in change. Help them learn how to cope with the new system rather than imposing it once the great plan has been worked out.

So on your next assignment who are the people on your list? How can you gain their information and support? What will you do to ensure effective consultation?

What kind of data do you collect?

The vital thing about advisory work is that one is continually trying to gather, absorb, analyse and help others understand information relating to their problem. In a sense therefore the best tool which any consultant adviser can have is a sound framework for diagnosis and analysis of data. This is not in any way to play down the other areas of feedback and reinforcement. However, these can only be done if the diagnosis and analysis stages are properly fulfilled. Let us look at some aspects of diagnostic and analytical work.

There are various kinds of consulting activity, which are all identified by the nature of the information collected and the way in which it is used. Very often people engaged in behavioural consultation are seduced by the client, or indeed often seduce the client, on matters of data collection. By this, I mean that they have not clearly thought out strategies in the way in which they are collecting data. They are therefore likely to collect data without a clearly developed plan of campaign. Let us look at these assertions and try to explain in more detail what is meant.

There seem to be four main areas within which a consultant can collect data as shown below.

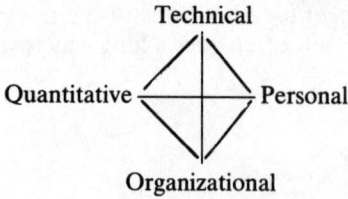

All the areas can be important. However it is important to consider what you need to know to help people improve. The tendency is to go for the technical and the quantitative financials, as these are seen to be the 'hard' factual points.

However, the real issues may be in the organization structure and relationships or the personal motivations and abilities. Therefore, in consulting, make sure you 'follow' the clients when they give you clues on what is important. Don't stick just with the technical or quantitative because you know those areas. Help the client work through the personal and organization issues as well.

How to collect data face to face

There are many ways to gather information including the personal interview, group meetings, questionnaires, just observing people, examining documents and so on. By far the most important aspect of consultation in my view is the time we spend with others face to face gathering and feeding back data. It is here that so much can be gained or lost in your approach. I have therefore summarized some of the most important points that I have found to be useful.

I have listed them as a series of dos and don'ts for easy reference. The dos are particularly valuable at the early stage of the consultation before you get to solutions. The don'ts are always useful at any stage of an assignment.

The dos

You should try and engage in the following behaviours.

- Reflect back to the client his or her concerns and feelings about the situation.
- Ask him or her to draw an organizational picture of those involved.
- Follow up his or her leads and let them describe situations with minimum interruption.
- Adopt a problem-centred approach.

- Encourage the client to come forward with views by non verbal gestures, such as a nod of the head, a smile, a lean forward in your chair, the writing down of a point, looking intently and so on.
- Use open-ended rather than closed-ended questions, such as 'How do you feel about the situation?' rather than 'Is it true that the situation is pretty hopeless?'
- Pick up the key words and emotional phrases that the client uses and give them the opportunity to elaborate.
- Support the client's endeavours to search for a clearer understanding of the situation by helping them to talk about themselves and their own role in the problem.

The don'ts

These are behaviours you should avoid:

- Don't evaluate and judge the client's remarks.
- Don't interpret the meaning behind his or her words.
- Don't put labels on the client or others.
- Don't contradict the client.
- Don't force the client down a conversational path which is of interest to you, but not to him or her.
- Don't imply, by word or deed, approval or disapproval of what the client says about others.
- Don't jump to offering solutions before the client asks for them or gives permission for you to do so.
- Don't show impatience or lack of interest.

Ways you can respond

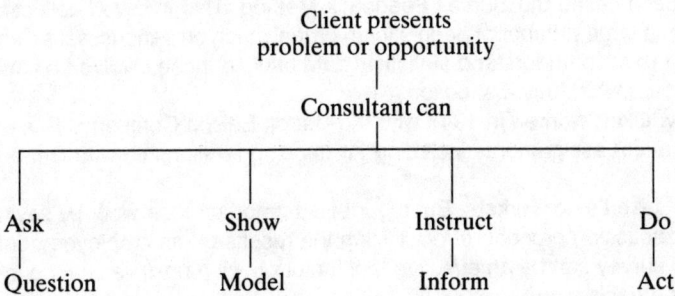

In any assignment you will be involved with a combination of these approaches. They should be used as follows

Ask and question: when you don't have a clear view of what the problem/ opportunity is and when you want the client to think through the issues for themselves.

Show and model: when you feel able to demonstrate what is required (as in coaching a piano player or conducting an interview) and you want the client to learn by imitating an example.

Instruct and inform: when you feel you have an understanding of the issues and you have data of relevance.

Do and act: when you feel you know what is required and the client does not need to learn the skills himself or herself, as for example when you employ a computer specialist to write a software program or you submit a report.

Where should you start?

Many organizational problems are open-ended in nature and there are many avenues which can be explored in order to reach a solution. Moreover, and this is vital, an adviser is not required to manage, but to help the executive whose area it is. Therefore it should not be part of an adviser's strategy to take that problem away from the client, but to work with them on a joint basis so that they develop a solution which is appropriate to their needs by working with the adviser. This is what is meant by *problem-centred consultation*. The emphasis here is on having the client do a substantial part of the work so that they understand the issues involved and develop a commitment to the solution arrived at.

Rensis Likert and Survey Feedback

We are all familiar with organizational questionnaires. Rensis Likert was a leader in making these the basis of organization consultation and change.

He developed together with his colleagues at the University of Michigan an approach called the Survey Feedback Method. This involved collecting data from a large number of people in an organization on various issues and providing easy to understand statistical data back to those involved so they could assess what they wished to.

Initially, Likert worked in 1947 with the Detroit Edison Company. This led to other major assignments including an ongoing relationship with General Motors.

One of Likert's co-workers, Baumgartel, summed up their work by saying 'Group discussion procedure for utilizing the results on an employee questionnaire survey can be an effective tool for introducing positive change in a business organization.'

Likert selected the following areas for assessment.

- Trust
- Creativity
- Punishment/rewards
- Teamwork

- Information flow
- Communication
- Decision making
- Controls
- Organization

In effect, it was a way of checking the organization health. This is now done annually by some organizations, such as Texas Instruments and IBM. If they see a dip in any area on their list of measures it provides a basis for intensive investigation and consideration. The survey is used as a thermometer to check progress and then action follows to bring about change if problems are found.

Likert however went beyond the survey system to establish a theory of management. Originally he identified four types of management culture or style called:

1 Explorative Authoritative
2 Benevolent Authoritative
3 Consultative
4 Participative

These later became known as systems 1, 2, 3 and 4. Likert provided extensive evidence to show that, in the organization he studied, those using system 4 were more effective on a range of business criteria. These included operating efficiency, grievances, waste, sales, safety and so on.

Therefore Likert advocated organizational change towards system 4 and the employee questionnaires and survey feedback where the process be used both to encourage and to monitor progress.

His approach has value in situations that favour the democratic style of management and his measures are powerful conditioners and reinforcers. However, the skill in making the change transition lies in the group process. The skilled management of feedback and the development of improvement programmes is the key to this as a consulting method for change.

Guidelines

Most effective consultation involves at least five actions.

1 Establish clear and attainable *goals* that will stretch the client and yourself and find out the data required for diagnosis and assessment.
2 Develop and implement a set of *processes* to achieve those goals whether they be training courses, reorganizations, new systems or a combination of these and others.
3 *Measure* the results as they occur against a plan.
4 *Feed back* the data gained to those whose work it is so they can understand what is happening and discover how to make corrections if required.
5 Provide *coaching* and on-line support guidance as required to help resolve problems as they arise.

You have to decide:

- whether to have an arm's length or arm in arm relationship
- the level of consultation
- the key actors and when they should be consulted
- the kind of data you collect and how you do it
- the best way to integrate action planning, action research and action implementation.

Exercise

The following exercise gives you an opportunity to assess your values in relation to consulting.

1   What are your strengths in consultative advisory work – action, research, action planning, action implementation?

2   Think of an assignment that went well and work out why.

3   Choose an assignment that went badly and analyse why.

4 Time management and contracting

'Remember that time is money'

Benjamin Franklin, *Advice to Young Tradesmen*

Establish a flexible structure

Consultant advisers are usually invited to solve problems or capture opportunities which are non-standard, non-routine and, often, outside the normal structure of the organization. It is therefore difficult to assess the amount of time and various steps needed to gather, analyse and understand data. It is important that you, as a consultant adviser, establish with the client a way of proceeding that, while flexible to the needs of the task, has a structure within which people can see themselves working towards specific outputs.

Developing a time schedule

The real difficulty in assessing timescales is the process work involved. It is hard to estimate the amount of time that one needs to spend in gathering, assessing and understanding data. I was involved in an assignment in which clients felt that, after an initial briefing, we should immediately begin our design in developing a management programme for members of the organization. On the surface, designing a programme does not sound very difficult. However, the important point is that any programme must be acceptable, otherwise it is a waste of time. Therefore, for it to be accepted, it must be based upon real issues and relevant to the work of the participants.

Within a few weeks, our team had collectively spent 25 working days in various planning and design meetings. These included holding workshops at which participants discussed their work; seminars in which we talked about the concepts; steering committee meetings in which we discussed the organizational arrangements; technical advisory groups in which we gathered specific technical information; and various other meetings which were essential to the operation. At this stage we had hardly begun the assignment. Nevertheless a considerable amount of time and energy had been spent.

Identify outputs against time

In a case such as this where there is no specific available technique, method, or product which is going to solve the problem, it is necessary to budget timescales. These may be arbitrary at the beginning, but at least they give some structure. One of the most important aspects of time planning is to set various dates for outputs. It may be a date for a report, date for a prototype testing of some aspects of the work, or a date for steering committee meetings to gather particular information. In this way, one can begin to structure an otherwise unwieldly project. This is what I believe is the basis for the success of a consultancy advisory assignment.

There is an important diverging set of creative activities and running alongside these and interlinked with them is the converging aspect of the timetable structure. My own experience is that people rarely give enough time to the planning and the diagnostic phases. Invariably these phases take far more time than the actual analysis, planning and delivery.

The early stages of a consultancy advisory assignment are important, because it is here that the assignment is either made or lost, by the amount of attention given to understanding those who are involved. All of this takes time. If you do not take the time, people have less faith in you. However, if you are in a commercial situation, it is difficult to get people to pay for this time, which they see as something which is interesting to do, but does not actually produce a result.

Commitment planning

These early stages set the scene for what is to come. They provide the basis for the formal and informal contracts of understanding. If this is done well it actually produces commitment. It provides the essential foundations to the project, upon which you can build later. I therefore try, wherever possible, to allow quite a lot of time at the beginning of a project. I substantiate this by having specific dates, times and outputs, marked along an agenda, so we have something at which to aim. These outputs are important for a steering committee, to show that, while a lot of process work is going on, there is a structure from which outputs emerge at regular intervals.

After having accepted a project and decided how to approach it, the consultant adviser must try to chart the way in which an assignment should go. In essence, what one does is listen intently for the factors which have produced the problem or opportunity. A client may feel for example that over a certain period of time work is not being done in an appropriate way. Perhaps deadlines are missed, or people show a low level of motivation.

Although clients can describe the past with a great deal of accuracy, they have difficulty in charting the future.

The skill, therefore, of a consultant adviser is to be able to move from where people have been to where they feel they should be. In this it is important to begin to develop the steps that the project will go through. It is one of the first things that I look for when working with a client, and the following questions can be useful in generating the necessary data.

Questions that advisers can use in time structuring

1 When did the need for this assignment first develop?
2 What have you done already?
3 Are some areas of the task of higher priority than others?
4 Where are you now?
5 When do you have to report to your colleagues?
6 How are things different now from what they have been?
7 What are the critical dates you must meet?

A management development example

A good example of time and sequence structuring is a project concerned with the design of a large-scale management development programme. Although the clients had identified a number of problems, they were not sure what they should do. They had visited other organizations and studied their training programmes, and had even attended a number of other programmes, both public and in-house, run by their competitiors. However, they felt that these programmes were inappropriate for their own members. Therefore, when we started discussing the project, they did not wish to commit themselves to any pre-packaged design. What they wanted was something that was designed specifically for them, but based upon a one-step-at-a-time approach.

Eventually we designed ten phases which they could see as separate but related. A quick summary of each of these phases will show the way in which the contract was set out in advance so that both parties could decide whether to proceed. The phases show how an assignment can be broken down into specific actions so that both you and the client know what will happen. A letter to the client set out the phases, saying that the joint steering committee would decide after each step how and when to proceed, given each step was related but independent.

Phase 1: An initial meeting with senior staff to review the training needs. A workshop with specific staff involved in the training process.

Phase 2: A further workshop involving representatives of the operating staff and union representatives, together with visits to their work situations, and the production of a draft report on their views and ideas with feedback to them prior to the completion of the investigation.

Phase 3: The development of an overall tailormade design to be discussed with senior management, training staff and operational managers as the basis for continuing.

Phase 4: The development of a full training programme based on the accepted design together with prototype testing.

Phase 5: The amendments to the prototype based upon a test programme and the construction of detailed materials for use on the final version.

Phase 6: The development of a 'Train the Trainer' programme constructed to enable in-company line staff members to conduct the training.

Phase 7: The delivery and the tuition of the completed management development programme.

Phase 8: The conduct of the 'Train the Trainer' programme concurrent with step 7.

Phase 9: The review of the initial programme and further amendments.

Phase 10: A retainer arrangement to upgrade and further develop the programme.

These ten phases are not exceptional. They would be integral to the design, development and tuition of any programme. However, set out in this way, it did enable the client as well as us, as consultant advisers, to check our progress, and also, if necessary, to assess the progress of the project at any time. In reality, of course, there were critical breakpoints. The client obviously had more of a chance to revise the project at phases 1 and 2 and after the prototype stage. Nevertheless, each of these phases provided a basis from which we could assess progress and redirect our energies.

The skills of contracting

It has been said that success is a journey – not a destination. It is often the case in consulting, particularly at the contracting step. One of the key skills in consultancy advisory work is putting forward a preliminary proposal of how the project is to be approached, what steps and stages will be involved and how long it will take. The assignment, whether it involves reducing costs, increasing sales, helping to improve productivity and efficiency, or to design a management development programme, will be complex in that one has to understand the organizational context of the problem. Therefore in the early stages one has to concentrate heavily on gathering information. The client, however, will want as soon as possible a proposal on how you intend to tackle the assignment. It is not always easy to be precise at this stage since you do not know all of the people who will be involved or the extent of the problems and opportunities.

Prepare discussion papers

There is a temptation to write a contract proposal before you have sufficient data which may then be seen as a 'take it or leave it' proposition. This is particularly so if the proposal is written in the form of a mini-report and put into a formal-looking folder. When it arrives on the client's desk it may be seen as the official proposal, rather than a discussion paper, to which he or she has to respond with a 'yes' or a 'no'.

Therefore, when asked to put forward a proposal which could form the basis for a contract, I do not send a mini project report in a binder or any formal documentation with official letterheads on it. At first, I take a very informal approach. This usually involves sending a letter to the client saying that following our discussions I have put down some ideas for further discussion. Then, on a separate piece of paper, with no letter headings or formal notation, I compile a document headed: 'Discussion Paper'. It usually starts as follows: 'Some initial ideas based on conversations held with . . . on . . .'.

Review of understandings and options

This document is not so much a proposal, as a summary or review of my understanding of discussions that have been held so far. Having summarized those discussions, I then put some alternatives and options to the client at the end of the report. Usually these alternatives and options have been discussed already and are not surprises. I emphasize the words 'alternatives' and 'options'.

It is important, at an early stage in any project, not to close down on one particular line of attack. It is important that the consultant provides the client with an opportunity to discuss various ways of tackling the task. I believe in most projects there is more than one way of approaching a job. It is the adviser's task to let the client know what the options are and enable the client to discuss which is best for the situation.

Once these points are clarified, you can then move to the negotiating step where details of costs and schedules are resolved. In the initial document reference to these should take place but not in great detail. The initial objective is to define the broad areas of activity.

A consultant's checklist for contracting

A most useful checklist for contracting at its various stages has been produced by Sue Morrell, who works as an internal consultant for the Queensland State Public Service in Australia. It is summarized below.

```
┌─────────────────────────────────────────────────────────────┐
│                            WHAT                               │
│  • What is the background to the request for a project?       │
│  • What is the client system?                                 │
│  • What are the objectives of the project?                    │
│  • What are the boundaries of the project?                    │
│  • What does the client want from the consultant?             │
│  • What information will be sought?                           │
│  • What criteria will be used to measure results?             │
│  • What resources (staff, financial, material) will the client commit │
│    to the project?                                            │
│  • What support does the consultant need to carry out the project? │
│  • What checks will be made on progress?                      │
└─────────────────────────────────────────────────────────────┘
```

```
┌─────────────────────────────┐  ┌──────────────────────────────┐
│            HOW              │  │            WHO                │
│  • How long will the project take? │  • Who is the client?         │
│  • How will the consultant and project │  • Who will be on the project team? │
│    team work?               │  • Who must agree to the contract? │
│  • How much time will the client com- │  • Who should be involved in dis- │
│    mit to the project?      │    cussions?                     │
│  • How will information be com- │  • Who should be kept informed of │
│    municated?               │    progress?                     │
│  • How will confidentiality be main- │                          │
│    tained?                  │                                  │
└─────────────────────────────┘  └──────────────────────────────┘
```

```
┌──────────────────┐  ┌──────────────────┐  ┌──────────────────┐
│      WHEN        │  │       WHY        │  │     WHERE        │
│ • When will the project │ • Why has the consul- │ • Where will meetings │
│   start and finish? │   tant been asked to │   be held?         │
│ • When will checks on │   assist?         │ • Where will the con- │
│   progress occur? │                    │   sultant work?    │
└──────────────────┘  └──────────────────┘  └──────────────────┘
```

When putting forward a proposal of how you, as consultant adviser, intend to deal with a problem, you must consider these questions. Think through the last assignment that you had and assess how well these questions were managed.

The discussion paper is not just a proposal, but a clarification and summary of the issues, together with the options. I usually find that, as a result of discussing this paper with a number of people in the organization, we arrive at a position where the contract almost writes itself. That is, out of the discussion paper, the client amends and adds various points so that when the actual contract is written it has been done jointly. Many people will say that this is normal practice, and indeed it may be so. However, I must say that I have seen more contracts written as a formal proposal than as an informal discussion paper.

Establish joint ventures

In short, I believe that it is important to let contracts evolve rather than be the outcome of proposals based upon a small amount of data. In this way, the contracting process is essentially a consultative activity. It is a joint venture rather than one side buying a product from the other side.

This approach, I believe, is what is required in most organizational consulting assignments where the consultant adviser is concentrating on evolving a process of change rather than selling a product.

David Casey (1975) in a most interesting article put his finger on some of the most important questions in any consulting assignment when he asked:

1 At this moment which person is my real client?
2 Which problem is the real problem?
3 Whose problem is it?

These are questions you should continue to ask yourself throughout any assignment.

Clayton's consulting

'I want miracles for peanuts.' This is what one of my clients said to me when we were discussing an assignment. On reflection, I feel he is probably in the majority. As a result there is a danger you will end up doing a lot of free work.

How often, for example, do you find yourself involved in a contract, without being officially contracted by the client? This is a common situation, which can be dealt with simply by being aware of your predicament.

A number of years ago, a company called Clayton's brought out a series of drinks which were free of alcohol. The idea was to persuade people to consume these drinks instead of the existing alcoholic beverages. The drinks looked the same as alcoholic drinks and, in some cases, tasted similar. Clayton's adopted the marketing slogan that theirs was 'the drink you have when you're not having a drink'.

This led to a series of comparisons in various fields. For example, we had Clayton's negotiations – the negotiations you have when you're not negotiating. We had a Clayton's competition – the competition you have when you're not competing. Of course there was the Clayton's strike for the strike you have when you're not on strike. Best of all there was Clayton's work – the work you do when you're not working.

How Clayton's consulting operates

It seems to me that on many occasions I have been involved in Clayton's consulting. In essence this has been the consulting that I have done when I was not officially contracted as a consultant. I can remember one particular example when I was contacted by an associate, who said he had a contract with a public organization to design and develop some training programmes. He said he would like me to do some process consultation, as there were a number of political differences between the clients. We talked for quite a while about the personalities and problems involved. He then said he would send me a draft paper which he was preparing for the clients, to gain my comments.

I read this and then spoke to him again on the telephone, giving him my views and advice. He said he would talk to the clients and seek to involve me. A few days later, one of the clients telephoned and spoke for about half an hour, outlining the issues involved, and gathering my views on the role that I could play. She said she felt that the job could be done in about two hours and offered a nominal fee. In return, I said that a job of this nature, with the preparation involved, the travel, the conduct of the workshop, and any follow-up work by way of a report, would take at least two days. She said she had budget problems but would talk it over with her colleagues.

I then spoke to the associate who had originally suggested I become involved in this contract. Another half-hour was spent on the telephone going over the various issues, during which time I suggested it might be useful if the principal parties met me over a lunchtime discussion.

Within an hour, I received yet another telephone call from a different person, also from the same organization, who wanted to talk about the assignment. This telephone call again took half an hour.

As a result of this, the associate who made the first contact arranged a meeting for all the parties, including myself. We met, but the situation was still inconclusive.

By now I was definitely in a Clayton's consulting assignment. I had spent nearly two hours on the telephone, and had worked on the proposal document that my associate had sent me, but as far as the client was concerned I had no contract with them, and certainly was not involved as a consultant. However, there is no doubt in my mind that, as a result of all these discussions, we had begun to clarify a number of important issues about how the project should proceed. In fact, my associate was quite open when he said that he would like to incorporate a number of points that I had made in his proposal document.

We are all involved in Clayton's consulting from time to time. Some people may call it the selling phase of actually securing a consulting contract. But where does selling finish and work begin? I suppose it is when you start to be paid for your contribution.

How to resolve Clayton contracts

Another colleague of mine decided one day to resolve such Clayton's matters before they took up too much of his time and energy. He took the medical and accounting view that if someone wanted to talk to him professionally then they had to recognize that they would have to pay for whatever services he offered from the first meeting. He therefore said to people, when they contacted him, that they could have an appointment and that he would be charging them from the initial meeting. He was well established and had a number of big commitments which made his time precious. He may have lost some consulting contracts, but those people who did come to see him were aware that they were not on a Clayton's consulting deal.

To what extent do you do Clayton's consulting? Or do you work on a pay-as-you-go basis, as do other professions such as doctors, dentists, lawyers, accountants and others, and charge accordingly for the time involved? I have never been so direct as to do this, although I have felt on numerous occasions that I have been asked to give my time without recognition from the client as to the cost involved.

There are of course times when I am willing to engage in a Clayton's consulting contract. For example, I am asked to speak at various lunches and dinners on management issues. These are usually events where people are paying to attend but the speaker is asked to donate his services free as it is often seen as a marketing opportunity. However, all such events take time to prepare the speech, to travel to the location, meeting the people and so on. Therefore, I have adopted a policy of asking the organizers to give a donation to charity when I speak at such events. This is a halfway house on the Clayton's consulting contract. I do it free but the charity of my choice – usually a children's charity – benefits from my contribution.

Informal consultations

I have been involved in numerous assignments where the information necessary to get to the root of the problem has not been available in the formal meetings that have taken place. However, I have obtained extremely valuable information when meeting the people involved outside the formal arena. Very often this important information emerges in private discussions over a drink, whether it be alcohol or a fruit juice or coffee. I always regard 'Bar Work' as being as important as, if not more important than, the formal discussions.

The importance of bar work is nowhere more clearly seen than when one is running management education programmes. Although there is a formal arena for the discussion of issues during the teaching sessions, I am always impressed by the number of people who raise personal and particular issues in the privacy of the bar. This is not surprising given the fact that people are normally reluctant to talk about their own particular case in a wider environment.

This has ranged in my own experience from people telling me important information about criminal activity, through to hints and guidelines on how I should proceed in dealing with political alliances and associated problems concerned with organizational change. The important thing within such meetings is not to be shocked by what you hear, but to understand that the other person is providing information and to appreciate his reasons for doing so.

Bar work is of course a generic term. I do not literally mean one has to stand at a bar. Sometimes you have to invent a bar or a substitute for it. Very often a client will say to me, 'We've got some interesting changes taking place. When it's convenient I'll outline what is happening.' Now that is a fairly strong cue. However, this conversation takes place in the middle of a crowded conference hall, or at the end of a meeting when you have to race off. So what do you do? Do you say, 'Fine, I look forward to hearing from you,' and leave it at that? Well, if you do, forget it, because your potential client might also. Instead, invent a 'bar meeting' by inviting him to lunch on a specified date or suggest you give him a ring tomorrow. Don't let the cue go unnoticed even though a bar may not be available.

Bar work can be time consuming. It also invariably comes at the end of a day when one is tired and not perhaps as alert to the cues as one would be at other times. Nevertheless I believe bar work and the associated forums that people use for passing on private information are fundamental to successful work as a consultant adviser. Maybe the golden rule is to drink little and learn a lot.

Guidelines

Contract plans and the management of time are vital elements in any consultancy project. Timescales provide a structure of inputs and outputs, related specifically to dates, while project plans offer a set of specific steps which can be followed, in order to work systematically through the solving of a particular problem, or the seizing of an opportunity. It is useful in such work to:

- take one step at a time;
- keep the steps whenever possible small but maintain the pace with regular meetings;
- assess how long each step will take and cost it accordingly.

A crucial element, therefore, in any consulting work is the contract. This, I believe, needs to be based on in-depth discussions and I favour the joint development of a contract when a non standard service is being developed. In this way you and the client know what you are letting yourself in for when the action really starts.

A summary of some of the key steps based on a modified version of Peter Block's (1981) proposals lead to the following plan.

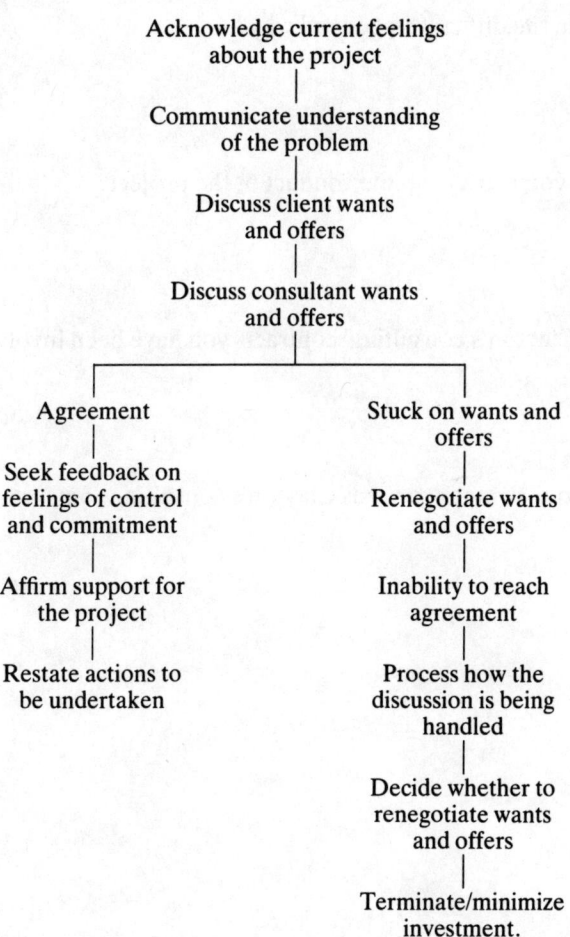

Acknowledge current feelings
about the project

Communicate understanding
of the problem

Discuss client wants
and offers

Discuss consultant wants
and offers

Agreement

Seek feedback on
feelings of control
and commitment

Affirm support for
the project

Restate actions to
be undertaken

Stuck on wants and
offers

Renegotiate wants
and offers

Inability to reach
agreement

Process how the
discussion is being
handled

Decide whether to
renegotiate wants
and offers

Terminate/minimize
investment.

Exercise

Consider the timescale and project plan for your last contract.

1   What specific steps did you go through?

2   What were the easy stages and why?

3   What were the difficult stages and why?

4   What did you learn from the conduct of the project?

5   List the 'Clayton's consulting' contracts you have been involved in.

6   What is your strategy towards Clayton's consulting contracts?

Part II
PERSONAL AND
INTERPERSONAL SKILLS

5   Interpersonal consulting skills

'In giving advice, seek to help, not please your friend.'

Solon

In all consulting work many words are exchanged. It therefore requires considerable skills in managing conversations. I refer to such skill as conversation control. In this section I shall outline some of the issues of how to exercise conversation control and be effective in the interpersonal aspects of consulting.

What is conversation control?

The essence of conversation control is your ability to manage your own conversation. It does not mean manipulating other people's conversation. The only way you can be effective is to understand what you say and how you say it and seek to influence others through your own example.

It is likely that if other people see you behaving in a reasonable fashion and exercising control over what you say, then they will respond in a positive way. There is no guarantee of this, but more often than not in a problem solving situation people will respond well if they feel you are acting in an understanding manner. I shall deal here with some aspects of conversation control as they apply to consulting and advisory work. A full description of the elements is contained in my book, *Conversation Control Skills for Managers* (Margerison 1987).

The cues and clues

The vital aspect of any consultancy assignment is identifying the key points as quickly as possible. This is not always easy because, although the client may be willing to talk about the problems and the opportunities, they will not necessarily be prepared to trust you with particular details until they are confident about you and your approach.

51

They will judge this to a large measure on the cues that you give them. If they feel comfortable they will then begin to give you some clues as to the main problems involved. You have to be patient and listen carefully for the important words.

People are usually giving a vital message when they use the words 'I', 'me' or 'my'. This is particularly so when associated with adjectives which stress 'concerns, worries, excitement, distress, interest, despair'.

Sometimes the clues may not be so strong. People may just say, 'I'm not sure' or they may indicate that there is much left unsaid, by a veiled reference such as, 'I've been thinking a lot about that recently.' When you hear doubts expressed or an indication that more could be said, show your interest and let them talk further. Don't make statements, or change the subject.

Clients will also give you clues as to the direction in which you should be asking questions. They may do this by emphasizing certain points or by prefacing what they are talking about with such words as 'urgent', 'important', 'vital', 'critical' and so on. These are the more obvious clues and it is more difficult to pick up the words that don't have such a strong connotation.

Selecting the cues and clues

I am surprised how often advisers miss the clues given to them. This may be in many cases because a mass of information is provided and it is possible to be misled. A client might for example say, 'We have been doing a lot to try and improve productivity recently. We have had a committee which has looked at ways of saving costs and how we can improve the quality of our products. They have met now for four or five meetings, but I'm disappointed we don't seem to be getting very far. The committee has talked about training people better and organizing some problem-solving workshops. We have also looked at the possibility of conducting some experiments in particular areas, particularly on distribution, which is one of our major costs. However, I am particularly concerned that we have not developed a plan which we can put into operation. Time is now running out.'

The client stops at this point. Which of the cues do you pick up? The main theme is productivity, but various avenues have been opened from training through to conducting experiments, and a number of topic areas have been introduced from costs through to distribution. There are several ways that you could enter the conversation. Here are some possible responses that you might offer:

- 'Tell me more about the costing system that you have been discussing.'
- 'What ideas emerged from the discussion on training?'
- 'What sort of experiments have been tried?'
- 'What are the main things blocking progress?'

Already you have a number of leads.

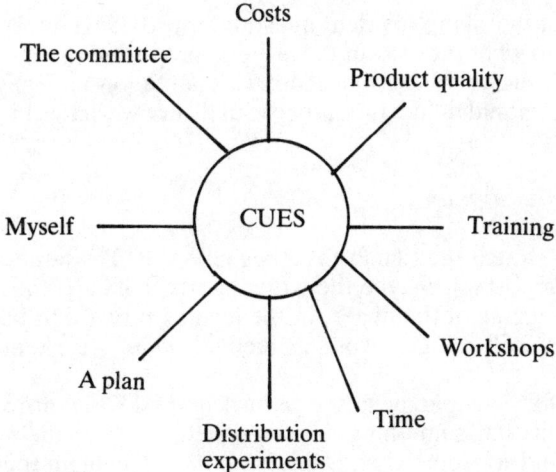

Now all of these questions may be relevant to gathering more data, but do they pick up the key clues being offered?

Follow the personal issues

A good rule in picking up important clues is always to follow what a person says about themselves. In this case the client says that he was disappointed. The adviser could therefore say, 'You mention that you were disappointed. In what ways does this affect you personally? At this point some vital information could appear, as the client would say, 'Well, you see, I am chairman of the group that has been appointed to deal with this issue. The president of the company has made it clear that he wants a report within six weeks and so far we don't seem to be making much progress. I can't possibly go and see the president with the half-baked ideas that we have at the moment.' Now by following this lead in what the client says about himself, the adviser has uncovered a whole new dimension to the issue. No longer is it just a committee working on a project. Your client has a personal commitment as the chairman of the committee, to the president of the company.

Identify listening cues

Pick up the important clues, rather than get lost in the conversation. In particular listen for what people say about themselves. Listen for the adjectives they use. Listen for the words that they stress.

Listen therefore to the emotional as well as the rational comments. Summarize the emotions. Seek to understand, recognize and appreciate why people feel the way they do.

People rarely stop talking because they have nothing else to say. They usually stop talking to see whether you are still interested and whether you are able to assist by asking the right question or providing information. So listen carefully to what they say in the last paragraph and the last sentence. It will usually indicate where their centre of attention is. They may not know what they should do next, but they usually know what is important.

The signs and the signals

Also, of course, watch the signals that they give you. The non verbal clues can be just as important: maybe the wringing of the hands, the shaking of the head, the wagging of the finger, or the leaning forward or backward in the chair. They will all give you an idea of what the client thinks is important.

If the client, for example, begins to sit back and fold their arms, then you probably suspect that something has happened to make them defensive and perhaps withdraw somewhat. If this is so, then you might reflect on this behaviour. Equally, if a person starts leaning forward and talking more quickly you can usually assume that they feel quite excited about the issues. Do not change the topic of conversation at this point. Stay with what they are interested in. Do not pursue your own intellectual interests at the expense of their thought processes. You are there primarily to help them think more clearly, not to gather information for your own personal satisfaction.

The cues and clues you give your client and the ones he or she will give you are vital to the development of a successful consulting relationship. Listen carefully to what they say and how they behave and then follow up, particularly on the personal aspects, and you won't go far wrong.

What managerial consultants want to develop

On a recent managerial consulting course for executives with a large oil company, I asked them what they personally wanted to gain. Most of their replies, as shown below, indicate the importance placed on interpersonal skills.

- More confidence in group situations.
- How to present ideas to others.
- Saving time and making life easier.
- Management of interviews.
- Communication skills.
- Improved skills in managing change.
- How to introduce new methods without upsetting people.
- Persuading others to take action.
- Listening to and understanding other parties' problems.
- Getting ideas across in a manner that wins acceptance.
- Saying no in non threatening manner.
- Getting people to work together.

Problem-centred and solution-centred behaviour

In most consulting assignments people are naturally looking for solutions. They will often form the problem in such a way that they ask directly for a solution. However, I have found that if you give them one too quickly, even if it is correct, they will normally find some reason why it won't work. There are two elements therefore to any effective consultation. These are problem-centred action, and solution-centred action.

Identifying the problems

In any consulting situation, we have to assess how much time we should give to looking at the problem before we start coming up with solutions. In some professions the time element can be critical. For example, we normally expect our doctors to give a problem-centred diagnosis and move towards a solution within about five to ten minutes. If they cannot come up with an identification of the problem and provide some prescription within that time, we normally begin to worry. If we were not feeling particularly ill before the diagnosis, then we certainly start to sweat and our blood pressure will probably increase the longer the assessment goes on.

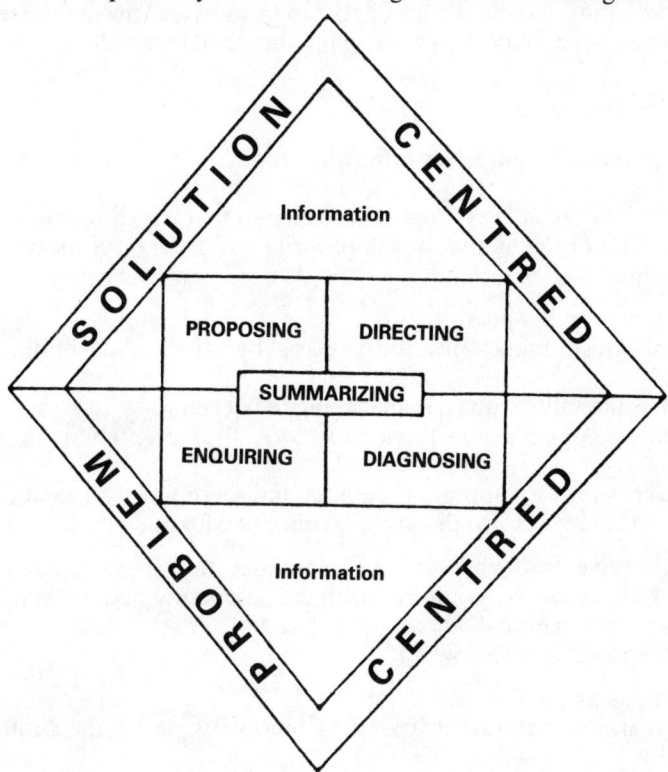

However, in looking at organizational problems we usually have more time. The client may be rather impatient, or just be wanting to see how you respond when they ask for solutions. They may come up with a series of proposals like the following. 'For a while now our managers have not been performing very effectively. What do you think we should do?'

You may suggest that it is important for you to gather some information before you can make a suggestion. However, the client may respond 'Well, I've been thinking for a long time that we should have a top class management course which they can all go on. What do you think of that suggestion?'

This is a classic situation where the client has not only done their own diagnosis but come up with their own prescription, and in medical terms would undertake their own surgery if they had the tools. In such situations they have called you in to be a technician to implement what they have already decided.

In such situations, however, you should resist the temptation to become solution-centred until you are convinced that you understand the problem and a correct diagnosis has been made.

Making an active commitment to being problem-centred is not only difficult but time-consuming. It requires considerable skill to gather data. In doing so, however, you should be helping the client think through all the issues and providing them with an opportunity to assess the judgements that they have made. Above all, develop the skill areas shown in the model.

When to be problem-centred or solution centred

It is important to look at these two approaches so that we know where we stand as advisers. For example, it is appropriate to use a *problem-centred* approach when:

- the problem is open-ended
- the client must understand the process by which the solution is reached
- the client is directly involved in managing the developing situation
- any solution depends for its success upon the acceptability of the details
- the adviser is only a temporary member and there to act as a catalyst, rather than trying to solve the problem once and for all.

Techniques to solve problems, like any techniques, are valid if used in the appropriate way, at the right time and with the acceptance and understanding of those who will use them. The 'take it away *solution-centred approach*' is most appropriate when:

- the problem has been clearly diagnosed
- the client has no interest in spending time working on the problem personally

- the client is prepared to pay someone else to provide them with a solution without understanding how the solution is arrived at
- the adviser has special expertise which enables them to do the job better and more quickly by themselves
- the adviser believes that the solution arrived at will be accepted and implemented by the client, even though the client was not involved in the development of the solution.

How to summarize

In your response to clients you need to make it clear that you are aware of what they are saying. You do not necessarily need to know every detail, but it is important that you pick up on a few words. You need to summarize regularly and accurately what is said so the client knows that you know what he or she knows.

Understand

Early in the conversation it is vital to understand rather than to judge. Do not imply by word or deed that you think that what the client has done is wrong or inadequate. It may well be so, but your job is not to pass judgement. Your job is to understand what they have done and indicate that.

By doing this you will show the client that you are following carefully the points that they are making. It is important for you actually to use words like, 'I understand that the two key areas where you have been working which have caused problems so far are . . .'

Appreciate

In addition you need to appreciate the way in which the client has been trying to solve the problem before you arrived. It is rare for clients to invite you in before they have made some efforts to resolve the problem. Therefore summarize what they have done, not in the form of agreeing with it, but in the form of giving a clear indication that you appreciate that they have made such an effort.

Recognize

Everyone likes to be recognized in some way for what they have been doing. Therefore, show the client that you recognize that there well may be difficulties, but also summarize accurately what you hear they have been doing.

If you can understand, appreciate and recognize then the client will give you good marks, not because you have agreed with him or her, but because you have taken the trouble to listen to what they say.

I had a long lunch with a client who talked a great deal. Much of the discussion was not particularly relevant to the main problem, I felt. However, during the lunch I tried to understand, to recognize and appreciate what the client was saying. At the end of the meal, the client said, 'I know I talk a lot and have gone round in circles on this one, but it has helped me think it through enormously. What I have particularly valued is the way you have listened and tried to understand what I have been doing, which is more than I can say for the other people I have been talking to.' As a result we secured a very substantial assignment with this company which lasted over a long period.

Avoid seductive detours

A common fault among consultants is that they pursue their own intellectual interests rather than tackle the problem. Beware of consultants who want more and more information that is not directly related to the problem you are presenting. They are trying to seduce you to discuss what is of importance to them rather than what is important to you.

A good example of how a consultant can lead the client up an intellectual cul de sac is shown in the following excerpt from an assignment.

Client: The problem is that most of our managers are not using the new computers, despite being fully trained. (Diagnosis)

Consultant: What software do they have? (Enquiry)

Client: We have virtually everything in our resource library. (Information)

Consultant: Have you got the new Superscan package? (Enquiry)

Client: I don't know. (Information)

Consultant: I was wondering, as I have heard it is very good. I was hoping you might be able to bring me up to date. (Enquiry for the benefit of the consultant)

Now this is an obvious detour, but it is not always so clear cut. Indeed the consultant's questions can often lead the client on a grand tour round the organization as they ask questions on scheduling, distribution, pricing, personalities, organization structure, pay rates and a host of other items.

But are these relevant to an understanding of the problem, rather than satisfying the intellectual curiosity of the consultant?

If you are the client assess your consultant by how quickly they pick up the cues you give and whether they stick to the main points. If they start to wander ask 'How does that relate to the understanding of the problem?', or be more direct and say, 'I don't see how this information relates to the main problem.' At this point restate the issue and if the consultant can't pick up the cues, then find another one who can.

Keep on the main wavelength

If you are a consultant then be aware that the client will judge you on how quickly you can get on the right wavelength. Don't take detours to satisfy your own intellectual interests. Stay with what the client says. Follow his or her leads. If, however, you feel this is not getting you to the point then say, 'We have covered a number of points; which of these is most important in terms of the problem?' If the client says none of them are, then ask for permission to widen the diagnosis by saying 'Well, I would like to broaden the area of discussion for a while if that is OK with you.' At least you now have permission, but still use it with discretion.

On most occasions you won't go far wrong if you listen to what the client says about himself or herself. Remember they are on a journey trying to reach a destination. You have to find out where it is and how they are getting there and what is in the way. That is the key. Once you know those things, you are on the right track.

Conversation skills in consulting

The following issues in conversation can be extremely important in advisory work.

Time dynamics

You can talk in one or more of three levels:

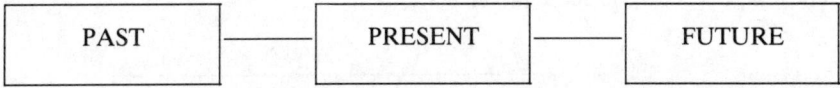

If you are talking about the future (what will or should be) and the other person is talking about the past (what has been) then you will not succeed. Many grievance meetings fail because the person with the grievance wants to highlight the basis for the problem in the past and the manager will probably want to be discussing what will happen *next*. You need to be in the same dimension to make progress. By recognizing the time dynamics in a conversation you can quickly move into the same time period before moving on by the use of conversational linking techniques. Your client may be fixated on talking about the past and you therefore need to ask him or her to consider future options. Alternatively you may find the client wants to move too quickly to the future-based solution before the past failure has been diagnosed.

Topic dynamics

What you talk about will highlight differences or similarities in approach. The five main areas are

- myself
- you
- us
- them (who are not there)
- things (e.g. the weather, cars, etc.)

Very often conversations fail because people cannot get on to the same topic wavelength. If you insist on talking about 'things' when I want to talk about 'myself', we shall have two opposed agendas going, and this is likely to result in talk without meaning. A sound rule is to get the client to talk about themself and their role.

Competition dynamics

Very often in conversation you can have a situation where someone is trying to get the better of you. The conversation becomes a win/lose relationship. There are four possibilities.

- I win, you lose
- You win, I lose
- You lose, I lose
- You win, I win

These options can be seen as follows:

		You	
		Win	Lose
Me	Win	Success	One up
	Lose	One down	Failure

Consulting should obviously be a cooperative exercise. Wherever possible, it is usually best to try for the win/win option. This is not always possible or desirable. There are occasions when you need to assert your views, even if it means others don't get what they want. Clients clearly want to gain a win out of the conversation, and there may be occasions, for example in negotiation, where there will be elements of win/lose about your relationhip. However, a win/win is nearly always best because it will lead to more lasting success and commitment.

Movement dynamics

The way clients and people in general react to you will depend largely on how you behave towards them. You can adopt one of three behaviours:

- You can encourage people
- You can discourage people
- You can ignore people.

As a result, people will move in one of three ways:

- Towards you
- Away from you
- Against you.

It is not only what you say, but the way you say it, that counts. If people are moving away when you want them to move toward, look at what you are saying and how you say it. Their behaviour is likely to relate to your approach. Likewise, you will find other people will 'turn you on' or 'turn you off' by their behaviour. By observing and knowing how to control your conversation, you can have better control of your relationships.

Direction dynamics

Conversations need at times to open out and generate ideas and, at others, to become more specific. You have to decide when to

- diverge
- converge

If you converge too quickly you may not get all the information you need. Learn the skill of keeping judgement in suspense until you have the data and the time is right to converge on an option.

Facts and feeling dynamics

All conversations resolve round these issues. Make sure you discuss both. If you are given facts, ask for feelings. If you are given feelings, ask for facts. In this way you will cover both the rational and the emotional aspects of the problem.

Level of conversation dynamics

You will find conversations take place at one of two levels:

- generalities
- specifics

You can move conversation to either a general or a specific level. As a rule

Gaining and giving information

In any consulting assignment it is important to know where the conversation is and where it should be. This particularly applies to the use of facts and feelings and moving the conversation from generalities to specifics. A useful way of mapping where you are is as follows.

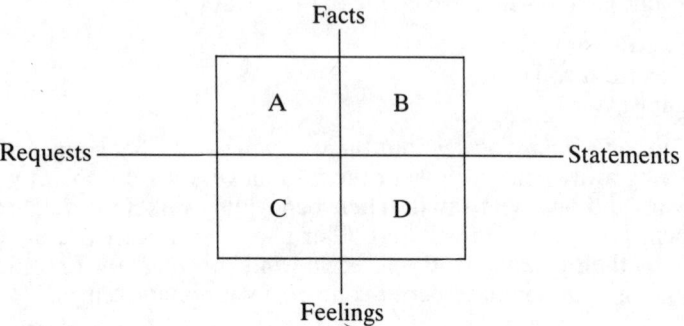

You may start out by requesting facts (A) but the client may give a statement of feelings and opinions (D). If that happens then accept that the client wishes to work in this area before you get to the facts.

Likewise you may ask how the client feels about the issue (C) and get statements of fact (B). If so, this is a strong cue you should follow.

Another way of mapping conversation is to look at the level at which it is conducted.

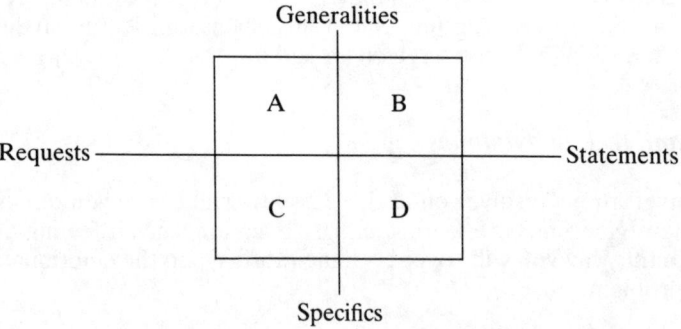

Initially in an assignment you will probably be presented with general statements (B). However, by understanding the principles of conversation control you can move the conversation into all four areas. You need to judge the atmosphere and not rush too quickly from area A to area C unless you have permission. People will only provide specific statements (D) when they begin to trust you. Keep your eyes and ears on the cues and clues.

we start at a general level and move to specifics. However, you need to read what the other person requires. It is no use you being general if they want to be specific and vice versa.

Agreement disagreement dynamics

In all conversations people will move for or against what you say. Be prepared for it by recognizing the movements on a continuum.

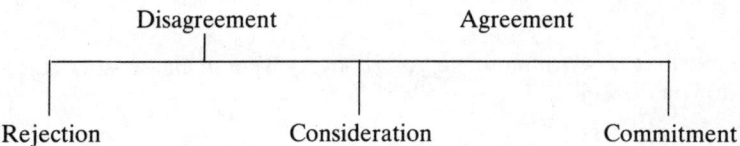

This continuum will provide a good guide for your action. For example, don't regard disagreement as rejection. Find out what they disagree and work positively on those points as you may get the other person to consider, then agree with, what you are saying. Also, don't confuse agreement with commitment. The first only means people will verbally acknowledge what you say, but commitment means action. That is what you must go for and seek to get in writing when it really counts.

You can be master or victim of conversations. You have to decide what words to use and how to use them. You cannot control what others say, but you can control what you say. In doing so, you can influence the outcome of the matter being discussed. The techniques and methods listed here are just part of the skills an adviser needs to succeed, but a vitally important part.

My favourite quotation on conversation control skills comes from Lewis Carroll's *Through the Looking Glass*, when Humpty Dumpty says, 'When I use a word, it means just what I choose it to mean – neither more nor less.'

'The question is,' said Alice, 'whether you *can* make words mean so many different things.'

'The question is,' said Humpty Dumpty, 'which is to be Master – that's all.'

Guidelines

To be an effective consultant you need to manage your conversation effectively. This will require knowing

- when to be problem-centred or solution-centred
- when to converge or diverge
- when to emphasize facts or feelings
- when to speed up or slow down conversations
- how to identify cues and clues

- how to summarize and move conversation forward
- how to recognize, understand and appreciate but assert your views
- how to move from the past to the present and future
- how to manage the win/lose aspect of conversations.

In all of the various conversation dynamics the most important thing is to remember what the client says about him or herself. That is the key to action.

Exercise

1   Consider how you manage your conversation in an advisory role. What do you do well?

2   What skills do you need to improve?

6 How to gain permission and territory

'If at first you don't succeed you are running about average.'

M. H. Anderson

As a consultant adviser you are invariably working on someone else's problems or opportunities. You can only succeed in so far as they give you permission to operate on their territory.

The concepts of permission and territory are crucial to understanding the consulting process. When someone is asking for advice they are not always prepared to tell you in the first instance many of the things you need to know. For example, a client may give you a little information just to see how you respond. If you appear to be negative or critical or lacking in enthusiasm then they may not tell you any more. They will find a convenient way of changing the subject and cutting off discussion on the important matters.

How far can you go?

If you show through both word and deed that you are genuinely interested to understand what they are saying and not prepared to jump to conclusions ahead of the evidence, then clients will open up a little further and tell you more of the details. In this way they will allow you to enter further into their territory.

It is something like knocking at doors which are half open and seeing them either close in your face, or open fully. It depends upon how you behave as a consultant adviser whether the doors open or close. For example, consider the exchanges in the two dialogues below, which briefly show two entirely different approaches and the results.

Case A Understanding the client

Client: I've been feeling under pressure for some time because things have not been going right. I made some changes to our distribution system about six months ago but there have been no improvements so far.

Consultant: You feel things could have gone better?

Client: I was looking for significant cost reductions and improvements in the speed of our deliveries. As it is our costs have gone up by 5 per cent and we now have a larger number of items in stock awaiting distribution than we had six months ago.

Consultant: So overall you are worse off after the changes?

Client: Yes, in financial terms, and we continue to have resistance from the staff. On balance I probably did not sell it too well when we introduced the idea originally.

Now here the consultant through a series of reflective summaries has shown understanding of what the client is saying. As a result the client has opened up and provided more information. The case is now poised at a delicate point. What would you say next to encourage the client to open the door further and give you permission to look into what they have done?

The client has given a strong clue that he will be prepared to talk about his own approach in making the change. You are now at a vital point. The consultant who is on top of the job will follow this immediately and ask the client to talk about what they have done, how they did it and what they felt about the situation and this would be preparatory for discussing what they should do next.

Case B Misguided consultation

However, a consultant who was behaving in an ineffective way might respond in the following manner. The result is the doors would be shut and permission withdrawn so you could not go further.

Client: We had some sound proposals but we could not implement them.

Consultant: It looks to me that you made some mistakes in communication.

Client: The changes were well researched before we put them into operation and everyone was formally notified.

Consultant: But you failed to get the commitment of the people to the changes.

Client: That's easy to say in hindsight, but at the time we were under a lot of pressure.

Already the client is becoming defensive and making excuses and explanations. The consultant has forced the client onto the defensive.

Instead of talking about how the problem can be resolved now and in the future, the discussion has reverted to the past. Already the client is starting to withdraw permission and will shortly move to cut down the territory where the consultant can operate.

It is therefore very important to be aware of the cues and clues that you get and know how to respond. If you can pick them up and work with the key words, phrases and ideas, then you will find the clients will invariably move towards you rather than away.

They will start talking more about themselves and their own role in proceedings. Instead of emphasizing the problems of the past they will talk about the concerns of the present and what needs to be done in the future.

Giving and gaining permissions

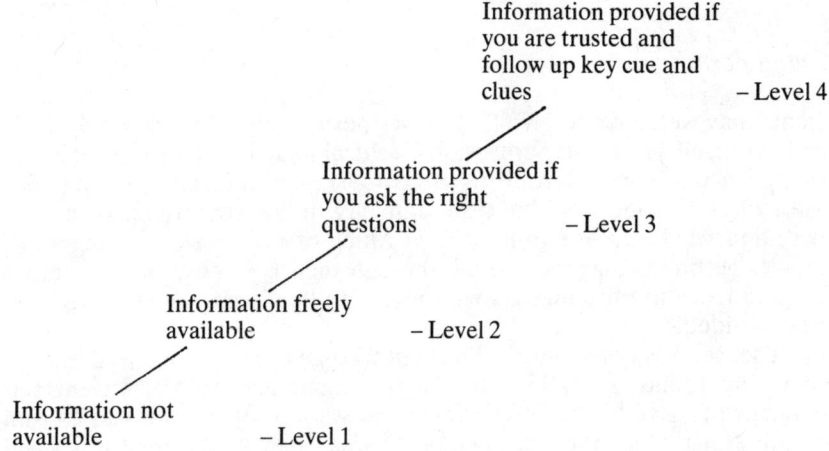

Information provided if you are trusted and follow up key cue and clues — Level 4

Information provided if you ask the right questions — Level 3

Information freely available — Level 2

Information not available — Level 1

Who, what, when and how

In order to make progress you need to find out who the client needs to talk to, what they need to talk about and how that should be structured. In doing this you will be exploring the new territory on which they must move if they are to be successful. I take notice when one of my clients suggests that I should meet someone else in their organization.

What they are saying at this point is that I have permission to go further. They are prepared to open up another door and allow me onto other territory. They are indicating that I am *persona grata* and have their confidence and trust to meet with other actors in the real life work play in which they are engaged.

Gaining permissions

To arrive at this point, however, you may need to ask questions which are related to permission and territory in order that the client can begin to think through what needs to be done. At the appropriate time you need to ask questions like:

- 'Who else is involved with you in tackling this problem?'
- 'To what extent is it useful if I talk with them?'
- 'If you were to hold a meeting on the issue, who would you feel should attend?'

These may seem to be general questions, but they enable the client to think through the next steps and who they will involve. If a client is telling you things that they have not discussed with other people who they have indicated are important, then it is your job to enquire whether they should move on to that territory.

Giving permissions

Clients may well have to give themselves permission. The whole notion of giving yourself as a client permission is critical to action. However, it is not easy, particularly when problems are complex and difficult. You may not wish to talk to someone about the difficulty unless you are clear in your own mind what you are going to say. Much of my own consulting work involves getting managers to think through their own position and gather the confidence to raise matters which need to be discussed that have been so far avoided.

In a sense, it is not so much the client who gives me permission, but the other way round. In talking to me the client generates sufficient self confidence to give himself or herself permission to open up discussions in difficult areas. Once this has been done, it is often a very great relief and they feel that a load has been taken off their mind before the discussions have taken place.

In essence what they have done is to give themselves permission to act rather than to worry. If you as a consultant adviser enable them to do this through your questions and discussions, then you have made a significant contribution, even though you may not be directly involved in those subsequent discussions.

By understanding the nature of territories and permissions and picking up the cues and clues in such a way that people can talk more openly, you are facilitating the process where people can become more confident in taking action.

Identifying the accessible territory

Closing down

Understanding permissions and access to territory is critical. You should listen for key words which will give you an instant clue that people are either opening up or closing down territory. Here are some of the expressions that I have heard when people are closing down permissions and giving strong cues that certain territory is not open.

- 'I don't think that's very important.'
- 'I can't see that working here.'
- 'We should tread carefully when dealing with such matters.'

Opening up

It is important to recognize when people will allow you to enter their territory or go further in a particular direction. Where people have been giving permissions they have been far more positive and come out with expressions such as:

- 'I would like you to meet Jim, my boss, as he would be interested in talking this over with you.'
- 'Although not many people know, I can tell you confidentially . . .'
- 'One or two things have happened recently which are important.'
- 'I'm not sure I should tell you but . . .'

These may seem obvious when they are written down, but when spoken they are not always picked up. The successful adviser, however, does not miss the clues which give permission and entry to territory. With practice you can begin to see more clearly the permissions that you get, which are in fact opportunities. As you respond in a positive and understanding way, you will find more and more doors open.

Why are you there?

As the 'doors' open up you may wonder what you are expected to contribute. There are a few rules that will help.
1 Listen carefully is the first rule. Perhaps that is all you are expected to do – at least initially.
2 The second rule is to ask the client what he wants. When you are on his or her territory it is not only good manners but good sense. Moreover you will quickly find out what permissions you have.
3 Thirdly, provide advice and guidance, but ensure it is wanted before you give it, otherwise you will find the doors that opened up will close again and your permissions will be withdrawn. You will be on the outside looking in, instead of on the inside looking out.

How others react to you

You can tell what reactions you are getting by observing people's responses. These can be summarized quickly based on the analysis made by Karen Horney when she noticed that people will move

- toward you – problem solving
- away from you – defensive, withdrawing
- against you – aggressive, attacking.

Now these responses depend to a large extend on your own behaviour and how that is received by others. In every conversation you are sending out messages not just with your words but with your behaviour which, as the model shows, will be encouraging, discouraging or ignoring others.

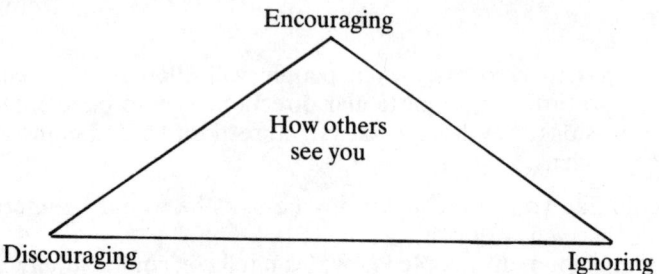

If we encourage people we are giving them permission to go in a particular direction. We do this in various ways. Some are to the point and indicate openly what we think such as, 'I think that's a good idea'; 'You have my support if you do that'.

Encouragement

Other forms of encouragement are more subtle. Just listening to someone in a caring and emphatic way is a powerful form of encouragement. It enables people to say things that perhaps they would not otherwise say. Asking open-ended questions, reflecting on important words or phrases, nodding your head and smiling, are all ways of encouraging people and giving permission if they are done properly. Equally we can discourage people directly and indirectly. Again the words and behaviours either together or combined are powerful factors denying permission to proceed.

Discouragement

I recently asked for some advice about music. My music adviser said the issue I was raising was 'irrelevant' and later said my concerns were 'not important' and went on in that vein. I got the clear message he was trying to discourage me. He did it in a manner that I felt was unnecessarily critical. Instead of discouraging me, he made me more determined to find out what I wanted, but not from him. I ended his role as my adviser.

   Other people discourage you in a more acceptable way by saying things like, 'If I were you I wouldn't do that'; 'Given the evidence I think what you are doing is risky'. Most people don't object to being discouraged providing there is some evidence to back up your views and it is presented with their interests in mind, and allows them to make the final decision.

Ignoring

The third form of response is often the most difficult. If people ignore what you say it can be taken either of two ways. Either they have no interest in your views and are therefore opposed and will not give permission to enter any territory which they control; or ignoring you they may be saying you have permission to do what you want providing it does not involve them.

How do you get people's permission?

People will not always say what they think and feel. They may be shy, or concerned that you will deride their opinion. They may just not be sure they can trust you. There are countless reasons why you do not gain the right information. However, it can be vital in your job that you do know what other colleagues and team members are thinking, even if it is critical of you and your way of doing things.

A top manager with whom I was consulting said, 'The higher I go in the organization, the less people are prepared to tell me what they really think of how I run things.' We talked for a while and I asked him how he encouraged people to do this. He said it was difficult because most of the meetings were formal.'

He agreed it would be useful to have a meeting on 'neutral' territory away from the office where his team could talk about how they worked together. I interviewed the team members before the event and found that some members did have strong views which they had never let loose in front of the top manager. When I asked why, they said they were not sure he would listen, particularly as a number of their points were critical.

I indicated to the top manager this general concern without naming the managers in question. His response was, 'I might not like what they say about how I run things, but if I don't find out then neither I or the team can improve.' He therefore organized a weekend workshop at a country club and in so doing signalled that people had permission to talk about his style and the way the team worked.

As a result team members 'for the first time got down to fundamentals on what was helping and hindering their performance'. By showing an example, the top manager had given permission for people to open up discussion on important territory. There was a feeling that this 'cleared the air and produced a better working relationship'.

Discussing personal territory issues

So if you want feedback from others you have to indicate they have permission to contribute. Often just telling people does not have the right effect. You have to set up the conditions, the time and the place and show both by word and deed that people have permission to do things. This is particularly so when you are introducing new and possibly risky ideas or for example reviewing someone's performance.

In most organizations there is some form of performance appraisal where a manager meets with each member of staff to review what they have done, to counsel on improvements and set goals for the future. Most people agree that this is an excellent idea in theory, but very hard to do in practice.

The reason for this is that it involves discussing personal matters – such as what you have done, or not done, and why. Many people are reluctant to open up. Some managers therefore ignore this and insist on moving onto the other person's territory regardless of whether they have permission. This is usually resisted particularly if they adopt a judgemental and evaluative approach such as 'I have noticed over the last couple of months your sales have been poor and your attitude to the job is lacking in enthusiasm. If you put more effort in, and take a more disciplined approach, you would be better.'

Now this may be true, but the critical diagnosis followed by the quickfire general solution is likely to lead to a defensive or aggressive response. It is unlikely the subordinate will give many permissions for the manager to find

---

Views on the consulting issue

Any consulting assignment will have a number of different perceptions and angles to it. Your job is to understand them and develop some agreed way of resolving any differences. There are five main perceptions in any assignment.

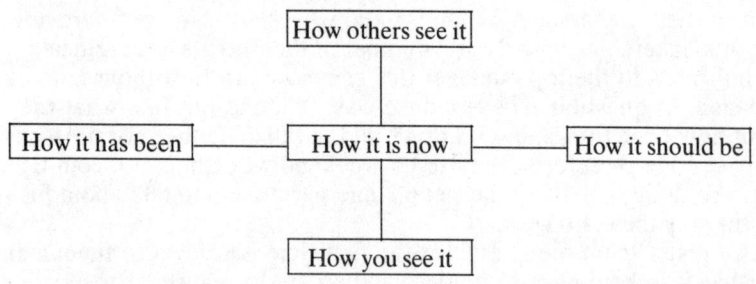

Your task is initially to understand the past and the present views. In this you should typically let others talk while you listen. A rule of thumb is that in the early stages you listen for 80 per cent of the time. As you move towards 'how it should be', then more of your own views can come to the fore, providing you continue to listen to the views of your client and those who must implement the proposals.

out what he really thinks, so how can you get people's permission to be open in sensitive areas?

The first rule is to give people an opportunity to assess themselves. The subordinate should be asked to write their own appraisal, which becomes the basis for discussion. In this way the manager can respond to the subordinate's points, preferably in a supportive and helpful way.

If the subordinate does not raise the important issues, then the second rule is provide some evidence for opening up the conversation in the difficult area and then ask the other person how they feel about the situation.

If that doesn't work, then the third rule is to say that you are concerned about the situation and ask the other person what they will do to improve it. If they still refuse to give permission to discuss the matter you may have to terminate the relationship.

How doors can open with permission

I met Frank initially at a conference. I was leading a workshop on consulting skills. Afterwards he asked me, 'Have these ideas ever been used in tackling problems in a complex technical area?' I was about to say yes and give an example. Instead I asked 'What sort of technical area?'

Frank described his own work situation and the problems he and his colleagues were facing. I asked what had been done so far and who had done it. As the discussion proceeded, it became clear there was far more behind the initial enquiry than was at first obvious.

'You see, we have already had one rather expensive experiment in this area, and it failed. We have to get the next event right.' I asked him what he meant by 'we'. He indicated that his boss was the key person, although he was the project manager with a group of technical people on a task force.

As a result of this conversation, he suggested I meet his boss. This meeting took place a month later and led to a meeting with the project team. I was asked to help design a new approach to their work and later joined in with the team as part of its development activity. I was then invited to meet with their international staff.

The assignment lasted on a part-time basis over ten years. It all stemmed from one short conversation, but as a result I received permission to enter an ever-widening territory. Each person I met opened another door to have me vetted by colleagues who then gave permission for me to enter deeper into their territory.

They made their judgements on various criteria, but most of all on whether I could pick up the cues and clues and relate to what they said. A crucial part of that was the questions I asked, rather than just giving answers, and that is why conversational control is important.

Process consultation

Edgar Schein first put forward the concept of process consultation. This stands in comparison to the technical content expert aspect of consulting.

As Schein (1969) writes, 'The process consultant seeks to give the client "insight" into what is going on around him, and between him, and other people.'

He extends this later by saying 'as long as organizations are networks of people, there will be processes occurring between them. Therefore it is obvious that the better understood and the better diagnosed these processes are, the greater will be the chances of finding solutions to technical problems which will be accepted and used by the members of the organization.'

His book on the subject, *Process Consultation*, is a landmark book and has stood the test of time. In it he described a number of assumptions underlying process- (rather than content-) based consulting. Some of these can be summarized as follows.

- Managers are keen to improve their organization, but don't always know what is wrong and need help in diagnosing the situation. The manager must be involved in this so he or she sees the problems and possibilities for themselves and learns how to respond.
- Process consultation therefore concentrates upon helping to establish the most effective means of diagnosis and effective helping relationships by getting people together in various ways to solve the issues.

It sounds simple and obvious, but like many things in life is more difficult in practice than in theory. For example, the basis of any success is knowing who should talk to whom, about what, when and to what purpose to ensure some positive outcome. If you are good at this you are doing well as a process consultant. If not, then you may need one.

Working on the clients territory

The organizational problems I am involved with are invariably a product of the relationships within the organization itself. If you really want to help the client with such problems you must work on his or her territory.

Territory is an important concept. If one is to explore territory one needs a map, but the adviser working on organization relationship issues does not have one. However, the client has one, even though they may never have talked about it or written it down. The adviser should therefore encourage the client to explain the important factors which they see as influencing behaviour within their territory which relates to the problem.

Follow the client

This means allowing the client to control the pace and direction of the conversation: try to pick up the essence of the message and enquire further.

This often starts a historic review of the problem. It is tempting but dangerous to try and short-circuit this. The client often gives a discursive introduction to ascertain how far they can trust you. Do you show interest in what they have to say? If not, they are unlikely to let you know more of their world. Do they think you will respect confidences? Do they get the positive cues of encouragement from you to continue?

Follow personal issues

There is a pressure on consultant advisers to move away from the client's territory, particularly when the discussion becomes embarrassing or when personal disclosures are made. Advisers often fail to help the client explore such delicate aspects of their world. They push their concern to one side. If someone new to a job says, 'I feel I am not up to this job', or 'I find it really difficult to live up to what's expected of me', it is vital that you follow up the personal cues by inviting the client to say why they feel this way and exploring options they can take to deal with the issues.

Don't avoid the issues

The following are examples of avoidance:

- 'This is a common problem. I wouldn't worry about it if I were you.'
- 'Let's get back to what we were saying earlier.'
- 'I've been interested in what you have said, but I would like to ask you a few questions about other matters now.'

In each of these interventions the adviser seeks to change the direction. He may be well-intentioned but each of these interventions is destined to break the thread of a client's narrative.

The first plays down the client's concerns. The second pushes him back to some earlier topic. Lastly, the adviser seeks to control the meeting by proposing 'a few questions'.

Exploring the client's territory means concentrating on what he or she says. It means denying one's own personal interest. It means foregoing one's own experience on similar issues, unless that is requested. It means following the client's logic so that he or she begins to see their own logic more clearly.

How to behave on client's territory

Remember you are always a guest. Never outstay your welcome. Never give cause for the client (host) to be embarrassed in front of others. If you have important things to say to the client, get their agreement before launching forth, or do it in private.

You can be excluded from territory just as easily as you can be included.

The phone will not ring, and letters don't get answered. The important thing is to respect the territory of others. Work with them, not against them, wherever possible, to make changes.

We all have organizational territory. We don't mind sharing it occasionally. Indeed most of us enjoy showing friends and acquaintances our territory if we take pride in it. However, we all object to our territory being taken over. Make sure your visit is exactly that, not a take-over. Ultimately the client has to do the job, not you. Your job is to help him or her manage their territory better.

Guidelines

Permissions are the key to successful consulting. You don't have to ask for them. If you behave appropriately they will be given to you. The points discussed in this section provide the basis for gaining entry, but be sure you do not take unfair advantage or outstay your welcome. Don't trespass for your own benefit. People will allow you onto their 'territory' if they feel you understand and are willing to help. It is a trust relationship. Guard it with care.

Exercise

1   Consider situations where you have given people permission to discuss personal matters of importance to you. Why did you do it and in particular what did the other person do?

2   Consider situations where you have been given permission by another person to go onto personal territory. What were the circumstances that led to such permission and what did you do?

3   What points do you need to concentrate upon if you are to gain permissions as an adviser?

7 How to raise energy levels

'We are all wise for other people, none for himself',

Emerson

Consultant advisers often find themselves in a position where they are employed by one group, but have to work with others at a different level to get the job done. These other people may be sceptical about the assignment, particularly if they have been forced into working with you. In this situation, you, as consultant adviser, must strive to motivate people, by making the discussions as meaningful as possible and introducing activities whereby views can be expressed freely and vigorously. You must, in effect, raise energy levels.

Build on experience

Such a necessity arose when I was teaching a management programme for the coal industry. In all, there were people from eight different privately owned coal companies who held superintendent positions in both open-cut and underground mines. Most of them came to the programme deeply sceptical of its value.

On the first evening it became clear that they were suspicious of such courses, as previous ones had been failures. One superintendent said, 'On the last course such as this, I walked out after one day because it was not relevant to my job.' Other superintendents supported this comment by giving other examples of training and education which they did not see as specific to their work. 'A lot of management training is just talk and doesn't really get down to the practical skills that you need in order to do the job,' said another superintendent.

It was in this atmosphere that another colleague and I had to work as consultant advisers. We had been asked by the coal industry to design a programme for the superintendents to enable them to develop their approach to management. There was no way that these people would respond well to being taught in the traditional sense.

They made it clear from the outset that they were suspicious of academics and consultants who came along to try to tell them how to run coalmines when such people, in their view, had little or no experience of the real problems. They were of course, right. Academics and consultants cannot possibly tell mining superintendents how to run a mine.

However, the effective consultant adviser can be of enormous value in helping mining superintendents learn how to improve the way they do their job. The skill lies in raising the energy level of the superintendents to look beyond what they do. This needs an approach where the participants are encouraged to look at their experience and share it with others for mutual benefit.

Start near to home

On this programme, therefore, we included, amongst the other sessions, a workshop which had the theme of 'Productivity and Efficiency'. On the first day we asked the mining superintendents to meet in four groups of five people to pick out the main features which affected productivity and efficiency in the mines. They had no difficulty in identifying the important factors.

Thereafter, each day alongside other parts of the programme the superintendents were invited to meet in their groups and consider each one of the factors identified. They were asked to develop ways of improving productivity and efficiency based upon their collective experience. They shared examples and illustrations of what they were doing in their mines.

The discussion level gradually grew in volume and intensity. Soon people were staying on long beyond the ninety minutes allocated to talk about the particular cases that had been raised. Late at night in the bar, the discussions continued. The subject of productivity and efficiency was central to their job, and their success.

Get specific examples

By the end of the week when the groups reported back, there was considerable interest in the points made. Each group commented upon the ideas raised by other groups. Many points were challenged and people were asked to produce evidence of how such productivity and efficiency proposals could actually work. Examples were given, showing what had been done.

'In our mine we have been working on getting people together for ten-minutes meetings before a shift to discuss central issues, such as safety, and this has really had a substantial impact ever since we have been doing it,' said one manager. This led another superintendent to ask how they actually ran the meetings, and whether ten minutes was really enough. 'It's not really sufficient time to get a good discussion going, but it does enable the foreman to get across the points and receive any general ideas which he can then relate to my meeting. The important thing is that it is done regularly and people see that management is concerned.'

Explore peoples experiences

The realities, therefore, of involving people in productivity and efficiency were discussed. People put forward ideas on how to reduce absenteeism, how to reduce costs, how to get people more involved, and how to improve performance with training. All of these ideas were listened to, commented upon, criticized and developed. As consultant advisers, my colleague and I provided the structure for the proceedings and gave guidance on the process as well as inviting the groups to present their reports. Throughout, we did not give lectures, but asked questions, such as how participants would relate the cases back to their own situation.

At the end of the programme, the productivity and efficiency sessions were rated very highly. We had not taught, but the participants had learnt a great deal. We had succeeded by raising the energy level; by choosing a subject near to the heart of the participants. We had worked with them in such a way that they could talk usefully to each other. We had then asked for outputs in terms of reports and recommendations. All of this provided the basis upon which people could actually begin to learn from each other.

Mining superintendents who were originally sceptical felt the programme had been worthwhile. It had indeed been worthwhile because they had put considerable effort and energy into it. The role of the consultant adviser is to structure situations where energy levels can be raised and put to good use. In this way people will perceive what they can contribute.

Discuss real live issues

Raising people's energy levels is a key to effective consulting. Invariably, your clients need to do a considerable amount of other work. The consultant adviser has to organize and structure the assignment so the participants can contribute from their experience and in this way you can raise their energy levels.

The same problem of raising the energy level existed with the airline pilots and crew members in the case referred to earlier. Initially they were also sceptical about the need for and value of a management programme. They could fly the planes. Why did they need a development programme? They had a low energy level toward the event.

I therefore proposed we bring pilots and flight engineers together to discuss, 'What issues they felt were important in ensuring effective teamwork in the cockpit'. Everyone had views on this, and was willing to share them. Gradually their energy level began to rise. The more they contributed, the more energy they exerted.

As a result of this approach, our project team obtained valuable case illustrations and data that we could use in the design of the programme. Moreover, we then went further by asking selected pilots and flight engineers to work with us to write case examples and make videos to illustrate the salient points. Again the energy level rose because people could see this was a relevant and useful exercise based on their own experience.

Active involvement in development

Try, wherever possible, actively to involve the participants in the client's system in the diagnosis, the development of materials, the planning, the presentation and any other aspects of the work. This process will usually raise their energy levels toward the changes. Because they are involved they will be part of the change rather than having it imposed on them. They also will make your job easier. Above all, their involvement will contribute to the success of the project.

Signs of low energy levels

Some of the signs are listed below, although these are not always definite indicators.

- People lean back in the chairs.
- People yawning and doodling.
- Lots of side conversations.
- Defensive behaviour.
- People saying, 'You don't understand'.
- People miss meetings or attend late.
- Low contribution levels.
- Scepticism and cynicism.
- Playing for time with long drawn out procedure.

How to clarify expectations

No surprises

People usually have a low energy level when they are not aware of what is expected or what is happening. It is important, therefore, to condition people gradually to what you expect. This is not always easy, as most consultancy advisory work involves change. In the normal course of events, managers would not call upon consultant advisers unless there was a need for an extra resource to cope with changes which were either planned or forced upon them. Therefore it is likely that a situation in which the consultant advisor works has some added stress attached to it above and beyond the normal conditions associated with ordinary work processes.

In order to ensure that changes do take place in smooth and organized way, it is important that people have an understanding of what is happening. They need time to digest what is being proposed and an opportunity to adjust themselves and others to the changes. Therefore I try to work on the basis of what I call 'no surprises'. There are many times in an advisory situation where the client can be surprised by the way in which a consultant works. Such surprises can cause problems in the relationship.

Check the details

Recently I was involved in a consultancy advisory situation which proved difficult because participants were not prepared for what was going to happen. In short, they were surprised and therefore resistant to the proposal. I had, as I believed, taken the necessary steps to ensure that they would not be surprised. However, my discussions with the senior management to clarify the situation had not been passed on and misunderstanding began to creep in.

This is what happened. I was asked to run a workshop with a number of technical people in the organization, to gather their views on a plan concerned with improving the safety and effectiveness of the workplace. As part of this project, I decided to write to all the participants and invite them to respond to a questionnaire. In itself there is nothing unusual in this. However, I had not told the participants why they should fill in the questionnaire and how the information would be used. I had assumed that senior management would write a covering letter explaining the reason for the initiative. As it turned out, senior management did not write such a letter, but instead sent out instructions for people just to attend the workshop and to fill in a questionnaire.

When we commenced the workshop it was clear that people felt they had been pressed into it without explanation. Clearly, we had broken the no surprise rule. The participants were rather apathetic about what we were trying to do. They saw the questionnaire as a move by senior management that might ultimately be used against them. Their energy level was very low. As you can imagine, it took quite a while to overcome such concerns.

Essential ingredients

I therefore try to establish policies in consultancy advisory work whereby, as far as possible, we introduce no surprises. One important ingredient in implementing this policy is a contract which has a set of stages. At each point, the client and those people who are involved can see where we are and what we are doing.

The second ingredient in trying to establish no surprises is frequent and regular meetings so people can discuss face to face what is happening.

The third ingredient is a structure which will facilitate the involvement of the relevant people. This will at times require the setting up of steering groups, technical advisory groups and consultative groups. These are all essential in any successful project of any size in order to facilitate no surprises and the acceptance of change.

The policy of no surprises must extend to contractual issues such as finance. If the price of a project suddenly increases, most clients will feel this is a surprise and react badly. If, however, you can, through informal discussions, keep them up to date with the way things are going, then they come to meetings prepared and ready for changes, particularly when they are substantially different from what has previously been agreed. This is not to say that on each occasion negotiations will go smoothly because people have an understanding but it is likely that you will be in a better position to come to an agreement.

Talk first, write second

In one sense the no surprise rule sounds obvious. In practice it is difficult to maintain the close cooperation that is necessary to ensure there are no surprises. All projects move along at a fast pace; there are many people to talk to as you get involved and all sorts of unknown things begin to emerge. The only way to achieve no surprises is to have close relationships with your clients in every aspect of the work and to communicate with them regularly by telephone before you write memos, as the written word is always more acceptable following a discussion.

Equally, if you are asking people to attend meetings, then they must have an understanding of what you are trying to achieve and the preparation is often the most important part of the whole work, in order that surprises do not occur.

So look at your consultancy advisory work on a day-to-day basis. Ask yourself, whether anything you do will create a surprise for the client. If the answer is yes, and you feel such a surprise will create problems, then think immediately how you can reduce the surprise by contacting them as quickly as possible to talk over the issues involved. No surprises is one of the ground rules of consultancy advisory work.

How to avoid bad surprises

All good consulting relationships rest on sound contracts. These do not necessarily have to be written down. They are understandings arrived at through discussion and negotiation.

In some cases I will write a letter or memorandum to a client summarizing points we have discussed after each meeting. Contracting is an on-going process, although the original discussions at the beginning of the relationship tend to be the most important. When such a relationship is very complex, then it is necessary to be fairly formal with the contract, as for example when an architect is negotiating a large building assignment.

Even these contracts, however, have to include flexible elements to account for issues arising during the course of the task.

Therefore to avoid bad surprises pay careful attention to the contracting process. You are engaging in an exchange of wants and offers.

In organizational consulting, the client may not always know what their specific wants are. They know certain aspects of the job are not going well insofar as they are below budget, or have high absenteeism, or quality problems exist. Therefore one of the essential skills in the initial stages of an assignment is to identify more clearly the specific wants. This can only emerge if you are skilled as a process consultant in talking through with the client the situation in which they find themselves.

Don't rush your fences

One of the most frequent problems confronting those who wish to change things is that they want to go too fast. One executive said to me, 'As soon as I have got an idea I want to implement it and see it working.' This is a natural reaction, but equally other people will want to see the value of the idea before they commit themselves to it. In particular they will want to assess the effect that it will have upon them personally. Don't rush them before their energy level is right.

What should you say when one of your clients is wanting to charge off and implement the idea before other people have had a change to think about it? This particular issue related to a salary system. For as number of years the company had established a system for its non-union managerial staff where merit increases were paid for people who had, in the judgement of their superior, performed above average. The problem came, however, in that the merit increases were incorporated into the basic salary. The next year's increment was based upon that year's rate plus the merit award. This was beginning to distort the overall pay system and also affect pension rights.

I was asked to look at the problem, and suggested that the principles of zero-based budgeting be applied to the salary system. That is, any merit increase should not be integrated into the salary, but regarded as a one-off fixed payment for that year. The zero basing would relate to the merit increase system and the salary system would not be distorted. This in itself was a relatively straightforward separation of the salary system from the merit system. The real problem lay in introducing the change successfully.

My client had four other senior managers whom he saw as the main group he had to convince. I asked him if it would be possible to get this group together to discuss the issue as a special agenda item. He felt there would be no difficulty in this and said that he would 'put to them the suggestion that the old system be set aside in favour of the zero-based merit increase system, as this would provide them with greater flexibility and also reduce costs.'

What would you say at this particular point? Would you support the proposition he is making or would you counsel against it? To what extent do you feel this is the appropriate strategy to achieve a change in the salary system, given that he regards his other four colleagues as 'fairly conservative'?

I chose to counsel him against it. 'I feel it might be inappropriate to put to them a proposition at the first meeting,' I said, 'I think it might be useful initially to get their feelings about the existing system before proposing an alternative.' I did this because I felt that he was rushing his fences in a rather solution-centred way and needed to have an alternative way of handling the process, before the energy level of the others matched his. He was about to force a yes or a no and might have got the wrong answer.

Managing the meeting

Clearly the process of managing the discussion was critical to a change being accepted. I therefore suggested that the strategy with a conservative group of people might be to have two stages planned rather than one. At the first I suggested that he might tell them what the topic was – the salary system for managerial groups – and indicate that it would be important to gather views before considering possible solutions.

I was suggesting to him that he took a problem-centred approach first before involving his colleagues in considering solutions. In this way it was possible for the managers to be involved in the consultations and problem diagnosis, as well as think through some of the issues, before having to say yes or no to a particular proposal.

Identify key questions

I proposed that he call his colleagues together and put to them the following questions:

1 How do you feel about the existing salary administration system for managers and the way it works?
2 What do you want from the salary administration system in the future, given the business objectives that we are pursuing over the next three years?

He felt this might be an appropriate process and organized the meetings accordingly. This approach is useful in many day-to-day meetings. It involves:

- finding open-ended questions
- dealing with the past and present concerns before launching into future plans
- listening to the main points and understanding concerns of those present
- taking action on the points raised and letting people know the outcome.

Learning from action

Chris Argyris has occupied many academic roles, but has always endeavoured to combine research with action. He is committed to the study of real life management practice and feeding back the information to the participants as a basis for helping them improve their own performance.

The principles governing his work on consulting were set out in his book *Intervention Theory and Method*, published in 1970. 'To intervene', he writes, 'is to enter into an ongoing system of relationships, to come between or among persons, or objects for the purpose of helping them.'

He puts forward three conditions which he feels consultant advisers should uphold. These are:

- Valid and useful information has to be generated by the consultant and fed back in a discussable form to the client.
- The options presented to the client should give him a free choice, rather than the consultant providing the client with a *fait accompli*.
- Internal commitment means that the consultant should work to facilitate understanding and agreement amongst participants so they can work positively and effectively.

Argyris in his many works has shown the relationship between finding out (research) and doing something to improve the situation (action). This has been well described in his book *Action Science*, published in 1985. He summarizes the purpose by saying 'by helping client systems to engage in public reflection, action science can both contribute to general knowledge and help clients improve their practice'.

Therefore consulting advisers must know the methods and skills of the action scientist in gathering, analysing, feeding back and managing their assignments.

Guidelines

It is important to get action rather than just impart knowledge and ideas. To do this requires raising the energy level of the clients so everyone understands the issues. This will take time. However, it is best to raise the energy levels amongst the people in the organization so that they own the solutions. Otherwise you will find the proposals are seen as too difficult because the participants don't own the answers.

Patience is a virtue in a consultant although, it is particularly difficult when you are running out of time and money on a contract. You must therefore condition your clients to working toward objectives and deadlines while at the same time enabling them to raise their energy levels to commit themselves to real action.

I believe that in any consulting assignment you need to concentrate on the four Es.

Enquiry   Your first and prime job is to find out and help the client understand their situation.

Experience   This is what your client has a lot of, and more often than not it is relevant to the work that has to be done. Find out what has been done before and how it can be built upon.

Expectations   Unless you know what the client is expecting as an outcome then you will not succeed. Also let the client know what you expect, as this sharing of views is critical to understanding of the processes involved.

Energy   You must identify the important points quickly. Don't work on the low energy areas. Listen for the cues and clues on the important items.

Some guideline tips I have found useful for raising energy levels are:

- ask open-ended questions
- reflect back people's concerns
- enquire how the issue affects them personally
- involve people in doing something of importance
- initially summarize and also become problem-centred when difficulties are raised before moving to being solution-centred.

Likewise some of the personal points I have found valuable with regard to presentation and interaction involve the ability:

- to smile
- to be at ease whilst still attentive
- to have an open body posture
- to keep to the issues rather than being diverted and seduced
- to reinforce a client's self worth through your understanding.

Exercise

1   What personal strategies have you used for raising energy levels on assignments?

2   Choose an assignment that went well and say why the energy level was high.

3 Choose an assignment that went badly and say why people's energies were not used appropriately.

4 What are your strengths and weaknesses in raising energy levels?

8 How to establish forums for sharing and comparing

'There is nothing we receive with so much reluctance as advice'

Joseph Addison

Often the formal organizational structure is insufficient to cope with problems, and the consultant adviser is called upon to open the lines of communication. This chapter shows how to set up an organization structure alongside the formal structure to cope with problems as they arise, by facilitating forums in which everyone has the chance to express their views.

Interdepartmental forums

The following example illustrates how it is necessary to set up a forum alongside the normal pattern of communication if an improvement is to occur between people from different groups.

'You see,' said the sales manager, 'I've got a real problem with our credit control department. I am out there trying to increase our sales. I'm encouraging all our salesmen to work as hard as possible because without sales this organization won't survive. However, we keep having problems with our credit control department because, as soon as one of our customers exceeds a particular level of credit, they are sent a nasty letter demanding payment, threatening legal action. Now this really upsets me, because it goes right against what we are trying to do by way of building up a good relationship with our customers.'

This problem of interdepartmental confusion happens in many organizations. It recurs too often for it to be a coincidence. What is even more important is that it is not solved by the various people involved.

Question the obvious

I was asked to advise on the above situation. I started by asking questions. 'Is it feasible for the people from the sales department to get together with those from credit control to discuss the issues involved, say, in a special workshop specially convened for two to three hours on that issue?' The sales manager replied, 'I think it would be possible, but it's never been tried. You see, we work in different buildings. The staff never meet each other. The salesmen are usually out in the field and the credit control people are locked up in their offices. Up to now we have only communicated via telephone calls and memos.'

It may appear obvious to you, at this point, why the problem not only arose in the first place, but had persisted. Clearly, the policies being set in one department were not in line with those being pursued in another. The people concerned did not have a forum in which they could meet and discuss differences. Therefore, problems and issues continued rather than being resolved.

Special meetings

I therefore suggested that we set up a special forum within which such matters could be addressed. The sales manager immediately felt it was a good idea, as did the credit control manager. My role, as a consultant adviser, was to bring them together in the first place and to facilitate the meeting, because the existing organization structure had not provided such a focal point. Unfortunately, most organization structures tend to run in straight lines, apart from a few committees which are designed to coordinate relationships between departments. When problems arise that don't fall into the sphere of coordinating committees, it is important to set up forums which can bring about improvement.

These forums can take many different forms. Task forces can be a valuable forum. Here, a number of people from different sectors of the organization meet on a regular basis to tackle specific issues and topics. Even a training course can be a forum where people are given a project to try to produce some answers to problems which cut across the formal structure.

Inventing temporary structures

Even informal forums such as lunches, coffee mornings, dinners, or a beer at the pub can be effective. However, these are outside the traditional formal structure. All of them require people to give time and energy to something which is beyond the normal routine operations. It is here that the consultant adviser, whether external or internal, has a most important part to play. Most of my work is done across organizational boundaries and usually means inventing a part-time or temporary organization structure for the job.

Recently, I have been involved in a number of assignments where this approach has been fundamental to our work. For example, we had a steering committee on one assignment which brought together people from different levels, and also involved management and union representatives. I have also used technical advisory groups. This particular forum includes people drawn from different functions, in order to work together on a design which cuts across their specific areas of responsibility. Operating staff are brought into a temporary group to gather their views. In another situation, we used a consultative group drawn from different functions and levels to look at a specific problem associated with improving safety.

Give it a name

One of the most innovative of these forums was developed in conjunction with the manufacturing manager who wished to reduce his production costs. He felt that the existing formal systems within the organization would not provide enough time for people to creatively consider cost savings. He asked me how we could proceed and it was agreed that we should set up a working party. He felt, however, that we needed a distinctive name for this group so as to show how important it was for the organization. He called it 'The Ridge Group' because we first met at the Ridge Hotel. This terminology of the Ridge Group became a byword in the organization for innovative thinking in the area of manufacture, and an acceptable forum for lateral and creative thinking was born.

The consultant adviser has a leading role in helping clients design the appropriate organization forums. The word 'forum' of course originally comes from Roman times when people would meet in the Forum to discuss and do business. Today we need to think creatively about the forums we have in our organizations and how we can develop them to improve the work that is done. A primary task of the consultant adviser is not only to design and develop such forums, but to enable people to work beyond the boundaries and strictures of their traditional roles. The consultant adviser in such cases can be a line manager or an outside person.

How to start

When people ask you to give an answer to an organization problem, first be sure you understand who is involved (not what the problem is). This diagnosis is essential as a prerequisite to any solutions which you may or may not have.

1   Why not start, when somebody indicates there is a problem, by asking, 'Who is involved and how often do these people meet?'
2   If the answer is that they do not, then ask, 'Would it be useful to set up a meeting where people could discuss the issues involved?'
3   If the answer is positive, then start working out with the client what the appropriate forum might be.

Manufacturing costs case

I was invited to consult with a manufacturing company that wanted to reduce its costs. The manager asked me how we should proceed. I suggested he get his top people together at a forum. We had twelve people attending the forum. In normal work these people never met as a group.

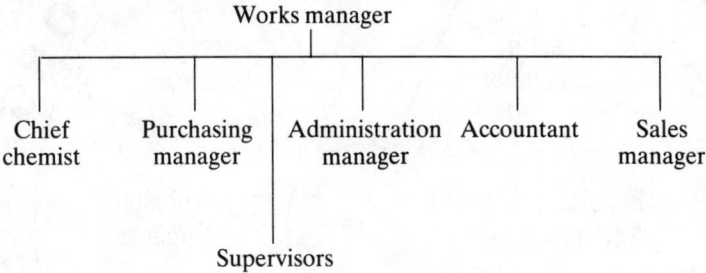

In this case my task was to bring all of these people into the same room at the same time to discuss the same problem in a systematic way. We developed many ideas for action with the result that the company made over a quarter of a million dollars' cost saving in just three months.

There is rarely a preset answer, but some of the suggestions and experience I have outlined above may be useful in developing a forum within which people can meet and resolve issues, which the formal structure does not provide.

Develop an effective team

Many of the problems that occur exist within, rather than between, teams. Increasingly today consulting and advisory work is a team effort.

This means that consultants who need to work together require ways of improving their teamwork. This may range from standing in for each other in a crisis through to a coordinated long-term cooperative project.

Our work led us to develop a special approach to team management. The essence of the method is to enable team members to meet and discuss how the team is working in the context of the members' work preferences.

The centre point for this is the Team Management Wheel (Margerison and McCann 1984). This indicates nine key roles which were identified from research with managers.

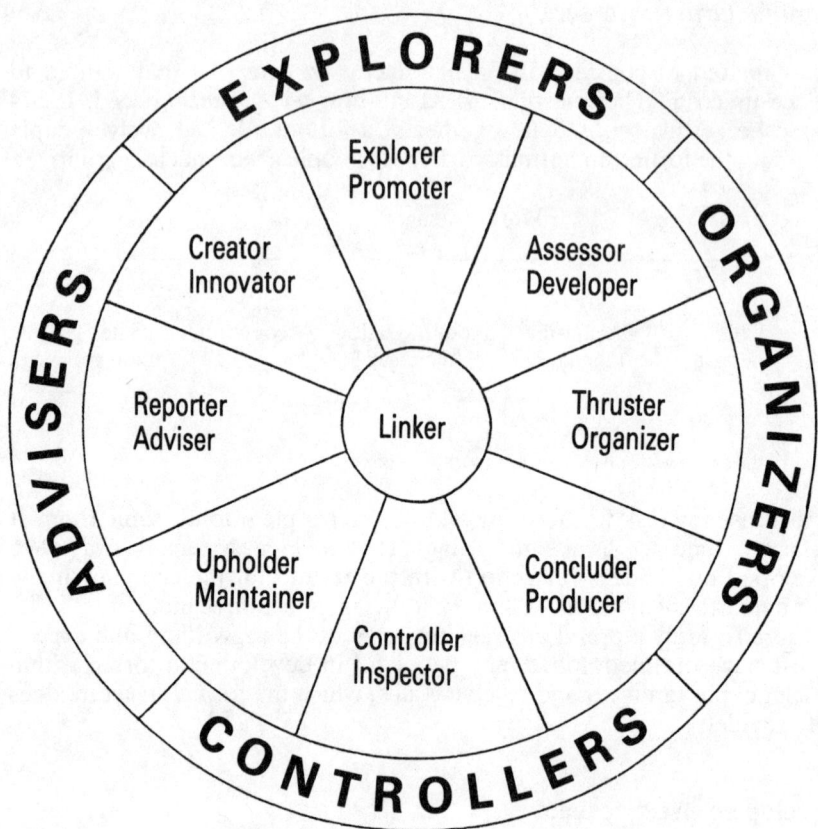

Team Management Wheel

The principal team roles are:

Creator Innovators: people who bring to the team the continual challenge of new ideas and desire to experiment with different approaches.

Explorer Promoters: members who are excellent at finding out how to make progress when there is no map, who cross organizational boundaries both 'selling' and 'buying' in the widest sense and representing the team often unofficially.

Assessor Developers: team members who are good at taking ideas and developing them into plans, prototypes and projects.

Thruster Organizers: people who like to set objectives and get things done by pressing the team for outputs and results.

Concluder Producers: members who will ensure the system works and like to run things in an orderly way.

Controller Inspectors: team players who keep an eye on the detail and ensure rules and regulations are managed.

Upholder Maintainers: people who emphasize standards and principles and provide the team with guidance and support.

Reporter Advisers: members who are strong on data collection and analysis and are the backroom planners and information source.

In the middle of the wheel is the linker role. This is essential in every team. This central role involves integrating and coordinating the work of others. It is usually done by the manager but other members can play this role as well.

All the roles, apart from the linker, can be assessed via a psychometric instrument called the Margerison McCann Team Management Index. This is a 60-item short questionnaire. It has now been used by over 4,000 managers worldwide. It provides a personal feedback to each person of over 3,000 words indicating their work preferences in the areas of information, relationships, decisions, organization and so on.

It has proved valuable as a way of enabling team members to share and compare how they prefer to work. Most members find it a helpful way of initiating important discussions on how to work together more effectively. One manager said, 'It has helped our team, all of whom have to advise others, learn more about ourselves and how we can make the best of each other's talents.'

One of the main findings is that most people enjoy playing three or four of the roles shown on the Team Wheel but not all nine, even if from time to time that may be necessary. The good manager enables the team members to recognize and play to their strengths. This is the way many teams are now developing. They meet to discuss how they can work better as a team, and the team management approach described here is one method that has proved it works in practice.

Organizations that have used the Margerison McCann Team Management approach to developing internal consultants and managers include Hewlett Packard, Shell, Kodak, Mobil, Citibank and many others. The team maps and ways of assessing work preferences provide a practical way of enabling people to learn from and with each other and use their skills to best effect.

Confrontation meetings

Richard Beckhard (1967) first proposed the confrontation meeting as a way of getting groups with different perceptions and interests to face up to the issues and reach a resolution. It has since been used in various ways so that managers can consult and negotiate with each other openly rather than fight political battles from behind closed doors.

One example comes from an involvement I had with the construction industry. A project had to be completed by a fixed date. The various groups on site were under strain and beginning to 'fight' each other. Some people began to withdraw their energy and the project was beginning to slip. The site manager decided to confront the issues. One of my colleagues was the facilitator. The process was as follows.

1 He interviewed the top five managers individually, then got them together to design a one-day confrontation meeting.
2 The managers were then committed to the design and invited their staff.
3 The one-day event had two-parts: 'What are the problems we face in finishing the project on time?' and in the afternoon, 'What can we do to help each other deal with the problems?'

In this way the issues were confronted and the managers and staff were better able to get the job done. As a result energy levels were raised and the project was completed to schedule.

Sharing and comparing

> ### The annual think tank
>
> One organization of which I am a member recognizes the value of a forum for future development. Each year the senior team goes to an offsite venue for three days for what is called a Think Tank. Here the emphasis is on new ideas and innovation in which the team is encouraged to think of tomorrow and consider what might be, rather than what is. The forum is outside of the normal day-to-day organizational arrangements, but linked to them in a positive way.

Petrochemical company case

A less formal version of a forum can be facilitated through a gathering in which ideas are merely shared and compared, without any structured agenda. This type of communication can be more appropriate in some instances for existing problems rather than just future planning.

One such case was when I had an advisory job with a large petrochemical company. The company had introduced a new approach to industrial relations, and was trying to encourage employees to become more consultative and pro-active towards industrial relations problems. It was felt that this would be better than the traditional confrontation approach where too many issues had to be settled between the union officials and management.

The company therefore decided to introduce a whole new range of work practices which it has agreed upon with union officials. These included the opportunity for people to take time off in lieu when they had done overtime. It also involved shop floor people having a greater involvement in planning, and other changes that required managers to consult with their staff. All of these changes required an in-depth understanding by management of the new policies.

These were explained to the managers and the staff in a number of half-day seminars and workshops at the refineries. However, it was felt that, above and beyond these workshops, it was important to enable managers to adapt to the changes. In many cases, it was not so much the learning of new skills, as adapting to a new way of doing things.

Developing an unstructured workshop

The company decided to introduce an innovative workshop. I was invited as one of the outside consultant advisers. The brief I was given was rather unusual. I was told there would be no formal course; no lectures would be given; there would be no skills practice sessions; there would be no films or video presentations and there would be no representatives of senior management appearing to give talks to the participants. In short, there was no agenda at all.

I was asked to facilitate a meeting of people for two days. The simple format was that the time should be spent discussing issues which the people who came to the workshop felt were important. In effect, the agenda should be created by the members. Yet it was not to be an encounter group. Those attending were engineers, statisticians, accountants, computer specialists, production managers and other managerial representatives from the refinery. The opportunity was provided to discuss how the new industrial relations changes were affecting work, and gather views and ideas from other people on what they were doing.

The advisory role

I introduced the session by saying who I was, and indicated, 'I've been asked by the company to come and work with you to discuss issues which you feel are important in the context of the various changes that are going on. I'm an outside adviser. I will not be writing a report for the company on what goes on here, or reporting back in any shape or form. The company has said that it does not wish to have any record of what takes place. The sole objective is for us to share and compare ideas, views and experiences on the way we, as managers, can respond to the industrial relations changes.'

At that point, I asked each person in the room to introduce himself and say what he felt it would be useful to talk about for the next two days. In particular, I said that any topic related to the work situation would be appropriate. We had eight to ten people in a group, and it took about an hour for us to make the introductions and outline the discussion topics that each person felt should be covered. I wrote each proposal on a flipchart list. This provided the basis for each person to talk about his issue and gain advice. The programme was a great success. I have outlined some principles I have found can be useful in such situations.

Advisory tips for unstructured forums

In the above case I fulfilled the following activities as part of my role.

Identify participants' issues: I asked each person to explain why he or she felt the issues were important. A whole range of topics was developed. One person wanted to find out more about what motivated people in the work situation; another person wanted to talk about how he adjusted his managerial style to the group that he had recently taken over; other people wanted to talk about how the industrial relations changes were affecting their departments; others wanted to be much more general, by talking about the communication processes within the organization.

Facilitate interaction: My own role in the proceedings was to help people to learn how to consult with others. In essence, this was a consultative group workshop. As far as I was concerned, my aim was to enable members to take an interest in the problems and issues raised by colleagues and to respond appropriately. Therefore, from time to time, I would intervene to ask how far the comment of a member in the group related to what had previously been said.

Generate conversation skills and energy: As we proceeded, I pointed out that there were principles of conversational control which could guide the way in which productive conversations developed. I stressed the importance of building upon the key words, listening for cues, and picking up points which had been unfinished. I demonstrated the way in which people could ask open-ended or closed-ended questions and how to practise reflective summaries. All this, however, was done in response to the actual interactions in the group. People began to realize that this was not just an exchange of views about the work situation, but an opportunity to learn some of the processes of consultation and communication, which they would have to introduce into their work situation more than previously.

Make the important points visible: During the discussion, we also visualized many of the issues, by drawing the main points on a board. In this way a number of the problems emerged as organizational system related problems. That is, by drawing out the people who were involved in the particular issue or problem, we could begin to see to what extent these people were meeting on a regular basis to solve those problems. On most occasions, we found that this was not happening and the individual usually agreed to convene a meeting of those who were involved.

Emphasize outputs for action: Overall, the issues presented by the members of the group took about an hour each, together with the group discussion and consultation. It was informal but concentrated on issues of real importance to participants. I asked each person to consider the outputs arising and outline their plan of action.

At the end of two days we had covered a considerable amount of ground. People felt that they had worked extremely hard and learned a great deal. A few commented on how valuable it had been to see problems from the perspective of other people. The engineers had commented on the importance of gaining the views of the accountants on some of their problems. The service managers felt that it had been invaluable to sit with line managers and to exchange views. Above all, a set of strong relationships had been established. People had exchanged personal doubts and concerns about their own approach to the job and, in doing so, had built up confidential relationships with others. I was interested to see after the workshop had finished that a number of the groups continued to meet informally on a regular basis, after work at the local hotel. They had learnt how to become consultant advisers to each other and create an environment to plan the basis for effective action.

The benefits to be gained

What was the outcome of these workshops? In essence they were set up as sharing and comparing devices. That is what I believe they were, and it is something which could be introduced with great benefit to a number of large organizations. The participants not only learned how to consult with other members so as to give help, but also derived specific value from the particular problem situations which they confronted. They went away with far more confidence about how to tackle problems, together with a greater sense of group identity.

The role of facilitator and consultant adviser in such meetings is crucial. The important thing is to provide an environment in which people feel they can speak freely. One needs to encourage members to follow a line of conversation and to build upon the key points. By sharing and comparing, they will realize that their problems are no worse than other people's, that their doubts and concerns are probably shared equally by others. Through group discussion, not only can they move forward in their thinking on how to deal with problems, but they can establish relationships at the managerial level that will continue in a useful way once they have returned to the work situation.

The ways hierarchy and laterarchy work

All these examples serve to show that the traditional principles of hierarchy upon which most organizations have been built are no longer sufficient. We have to come up with new organization forms of interaction to cope with the lateral communications that are necessary.

Hierarchic structures

The hierarchial system is still needed, but it is not sufficiently flexible to cope with the needs of fast moving complex business matters. The hierarchical system was valuable in times when business was relatively stable, with few new products, a low inflation rate, little competition, slow channels of communication and clear lines of accountability. In most businesses today, these conditions no longer exist.

The hierarchy also assumed that people higher in the structure knew more than the people below, primarily as a function of their experience. Today knowledge is so specialized that experience in itself is not sufficient to exercise control. Professional skill and knowledge has to be widespread today, and the person who programmes the computer may have far more power than those who have hierarchical authority.

The real weakness of the hierarchy is that it gets in the way of people meeting. If we have to wait for communication to go to the top of the departmental tree before it can go across and down other departmental trees, we shall wait a long time. Telephone, telex, and facsimile machines provide for instant communication and our organization structure needs to reflect that.

Laterarchic structures

This is why the examples in this chapter reflect an increasing move towards a 'second' organization structure. This is what I call the laterarchy. It runs across the organization rather than just up and down. It is characterized by forums, workshops, task forces, project groups, working parties, think tanks, conferences, temporary groups, advisory groups, committees and a host of other terms. Many are not new. However, increasingly they work in a new way.

The laterarchical approach to business needs far more attention. As yet we hardly have a language to describe what is happening. Increasingly we talk of networking and consultative panels. This reflects the move to bring together those who need to talk, wherever they may be in the organization structure. Some managers go out of their way to organize such groups by taking a 'diagonal' slice of the organization to gather views on serious problems. Perhaps the largest experiment of this kind is taking place in the Australian Telecom organization, which employs 94,000. It has established a national network mixed level group to develop ideas on how to improve the organization over the next decade. Initially they involved outside consultants to facilitate the groups, but now the line managers have for the most part taken over these roles. We shall see in the next few years many innovative designs to create a better laterarchy. In doing so, organizations will be creating a flexible system to go alongside the established hierarchial system.

Guidelines

We need therefore to create forums within which a problem solving discussion can take place, because the existing arrangements do not suffice. One of the most important skills a consultant adviser has is to re-configure the arrangements between people so they can meet and hold a successful discussion. This can involve:

- changing the location of the meeting
- inviting people who have not previously been to the meeting to attend
- setting up a special meeting
- ensuring that units or people who are interdependent but geographically separate meet regularly
- changing the physical layout of the meeting room, such as creating a semi-circle structure, so people can freely interact
- providing visual aids and ensuring they are used
- developing a design for a meeting that enables people to talk about the real issues rather than be hamstrung by formality.

These are just some of the structural skills we need to adopt as consultant advisers. In effect we are seeking to influence the process and content of the debate by careful structuring of the forum.

It is well known that sportspeople find it difficult to play well on a poor pitch. So it is with your clients. A central task of all consultants is to provide the right pitch and proper forum within which real work can be done.

Look at the organization in which you work? How do people get together to resolve problems and seize opportunities? Beside the normal formal systems for hierarchial reporting, what lateral communication systems over and above coordinating committees do you have?

For an adviser it is vital to look at the organization structure. The people in the organization may be first class with high levels of technical knowledge and a willingness to work hard. However, if the pitch on which they play is poor, with few forums for resolving key issues, they may not do well.

Look therefore to see whether a structural answer may be appropriate. If so, here are some organization structures you can establish in addition to the existing formal organization:

- task forces – short-term 'fire fighting' units set up to resolve problems
- project groups – people assigned to see through a specific project
- technical advisory groups – 'experts' in particular areas who meet to provide specific data
- steering committees – representatives of interested parties
- consultative groups – advisory group
- working parties – special groups asked to do a specific temporary job
- development groups – groups who have a remit to innovate
- creative groups – people who meet to 'brainstorm' ideas
- think tanks – off the job, often weekend, gatherings to consider strategic issues.

Exercise

1   What is the best forum you have designed to facilitate problem solving?

2   On your present assignment how many forums are you using and which are working less well than others?

3   What do you intend to do next to improve those forums?

Part III
PRINCIPLES, PLANS AND MODELS

9 What is your consulting model?

'Many receive advice, few profit by it.'

Publilius Syrus

We all have an approach to giving advice based upon a consulting model. It may not be written down, but it reflects itself in the way in which we consult and give advice. It is important that you know the model you are employing and are aware of its strengths and weaknesses. Moreover, it is also important to match your model with what your client wants. Therefore we shall look at four models which are regularly used. You may find that in your own practice you adopt different methods and can see your own approach in each of the models.

Four role models

It is useful to examine our work by comparing it with the work other people do. I have described the four role models of consultancy by analogy with four well known professions.

The models that we shall examine are

1 the doctor
2 the detective
3 the salesperson
4 the travel agent.

The doctor model

This is a very common approach, based on the medical analogy. The basic presupposition is that the client has some form of illness or disease which needs to be cured. Most people who use the medical model assume that the client and organization are in need of treatment. They start with an approach that concentrates on trying to find out the nature of the 'illness', looking for deviations from what could be regarded as 'good' or normal health. Indeed, a number of consultant advisers refer to healthy or unhealthy organizations.

Once they have identified the symptoms and made a diagnosis, then a consultant who is following the medical model seeks to find a prescription which will enable the client in his or her system to improve. It is here that the 'medicine' has to be taken in the doses recommended by the consultant adviser. This may involve an 'operation' to get rid of some offending part of the organism, or it may require an 'injection' to provide an antidote to the condition that caused the original problem.

I should say that I do not like the traditional medical model. Inevitably the client is treated as a patient who is not fit and able. The medical model further implies that the consultant is able to diagnose what is wrong and provide a prescription based upon some expert knowledge which clearly the client does not have. It also implies that the consultant has some knowledge of what 'good health' is and can help the client through the provision of pills and potions toward improvement.

This is not to reject the medical model in its entirety. Clearly physicians use this approach to very good effect, and our hospitals and surgeries provide facilities where effective treatment can be gained. The medical model is appropriate when there is a genuine illness or disease to be cured.

However, in my experience most of the managerial clients with whom I work do not see themselves as suffering from an illness or disease. On the contrary, they see themselves as healthy people who are seeking to improve the way in which they work. Moreover they do not look for pills and potions or a specific operation to cure the problem. They certainly do not see themselves in a doctor/patient relationship.

Therefore consider how you are relating with your client and to what extent you are using the medical model. There are occasions when it can be inappropriate.

The detective model

This approach is based upon the principle that something is wrong and there is a need to find the person or persons responsible so that they can be either changed or removed. The detective approach may imply that there is a criminal conspiracy associated with the fact that problems have occurred. If this happens, then there is a tendency to have a culture surrounding the consultancy work which is associated with blame. This may for example happen in the case of safety consulting where an accident has occurred.

The detective model concentrates on looking for clues associated with the 'breaking of the law'. Once such clues have been gathered, a case has to be made in order to establish accountability. Once that has been done, then the consultant is involved in presenting ideas and views on how similar incidents can be prevented. Those who have been found culpable may then be punished or provided with a scheme of reform.

The detective model has some strengths insofar as there are systematic ways of gathering data, and examples of this approach would be clearly apparent in safety investigations, work study investigations and some auditing work where there have been defalcations and other such aspects of consulting work. On balance, I don't like the detective model. However, I acknowledge that in certain instances it is a vitally important part of consulting work, if deviances from accepted practice are to be brought out into the open and corrected.

The sales model

Here the prevailing assumption is that the consultant has a product or a service which will be appropriate to help solve the client's problem. In short we have a solution in search of problems. This in many ways is the traditional view that many people have of the consultant adviser: a picture of the consultant with a bag of tricks ready to produce the right 'rabbit from the hat' to solve any particular problems.

Few consultants today would see themselves having this approach, although a number still behave according to the model. That is, they do have specific solutions and are only interested in finding clients who will buy them. They do not wish to spend time analysing the problem and designing specific answers to particular needs.

This approach to consulting, however, is beginning to change insofar as the sales solutions have a number of applications. This is particularly so, for example, in the area of computing, where a number of software packages are being developed. Consultant advisers trying to persuade clients to use these packages are usually involved in a discussion on multiple applications and the system adaptations that need to be made if this particular solution is to be adopted.

There is nothing wrong with having a solution in search of a problem. It may indeed speed up the resolution of problems. The important thing is to be able to adapt the solution to the specific needs of the client. I have been involved in this particular aspect of work with our development of the Team Management Index (Margerison and McCann 1984). This is a specific piece of technology which has widespread use in selection, training, appraisal, project management, team building and other areas of management. The consulting advice we offer goes beyond just selling the technology, to considering ways in which it can be best applied in order to help a client resolve a problem or maximize an opportunity.

All sales people are consultants. In order to sell you need to understand what the client is trying to do and how your product or service can match that. If you want to have a continuing relationship in selling it is vitally important that you find the needs of clients. Therefore the sales approach where there are solutions looking for problems is important, providing you can help the client with specific applications.

The travel agent model

It is this approach which I personally prefer in most of my work. The consultant adviser assumes that the client is on a journey. The clients may not always know specifically where they wish to go to or how to get there. It is the job of the consultant adviser to go through their objectives and work out the best means to reach their destination. I find in my own work that I spend considerable time working with managers who are thinking out new directions and wish to have advice from someone who has skills and knowledge of various options.

I do not necessarily recommend specific destinations where people should go, but spend considerable time helping them decide for themselves where they want to go and how they wish to travel. My expertise lies more in designing the vehicles we use. These include various forms of meetings people can set up to gain the commitment, motivation and enthusiasm of people. In this particular context, I help managers think not only where they should be going but who should be travelling in any particular vehicle. We may for example set up various project groups, task forces, weekend workshops or exploratory meetings.

Before doing that one needs to gather a lot of information, and be able to convince people that it is worthwhile holding such meetings. Therefore a considerable part of my work is involved in the process and structure level rather than advocating any particular technical solution. My job is to help the client with the process of getting from where they are now to where they want to be. It is up to them to decide what they do when they get there. I usually have very little involvement in technical discussion. Travel agents should ask where a client wants to go, and help them to achieve the most efficient means of getting there. From time to time it may be appropriate to suggest other destinations.

Maybe there is a good reason for not being involved. This is certainly true in my own case, where I have refused to work with a cigarette manufacturer whose job was to increase quantity and production efficiency of their output. I felt it would be inappropriate for me to advise on a vehicle which would facilitate something that I did not agree with, and the destination and objectives they were pursuing.

The travel agent approach to consulting is not so much concerned with causes as with consequences. Very often it is vitally important to understand the past and concentrate on the areas where the client has experience.

I have adopted a code that has served me well, called simply DVM.

D: = Destinations. Where does the client want to go?
V: = Vehicles. What methods are available for getting there?
M: = Maps. How can the client understand what has to be done en route?

This 'travel agent' model is useful in that it provides a structure to consider the main issues. In such work I can concentrate on both the content and, more important, the processes involved.

Choose your consulting roles

All of the above consulting approaches can be used to good effect. The fact that I prefer some rather than others is not to suggest they can't work. Each of us has a preferred way of working. The important thing is to know what your model and practice is and to use it appropriately. From time to time each of the four models will be completely suitable. The skilled consultant can pick and choose and knows how to change gear in order to assist their clients and maintain a high level of professionalism.

Having selected an approach that suits your purpose, it is important to look at the role you have to play. Consultancy advisory work tends to fall into three categories (Margerison 1978). Either an invitation is issued to work on a problem, or the consultant adviser suggests that he or she can assist with a problem, or you are fulfilling a specific role which has been nominated according to rules and regulations. These three approaches can be termed

- invitations
- proposals
- duties.

In most instances I am invited to do a consultant advisory job. This, in my view, is the most preferable way of doing consultancy advisory work. To be invited is to be recognized as a person who can make a useful contribution. Because you are invited you will, at least initially, be treated as a guest. An invitation also implies that the client is aware that a problem or an opportunity exists and is prepared to work at it. All of these conditions might change, but at the time you receive the invitation they provide a good basis on which to start. These three consultative approaches apply whether you are an internal or an external consultant.

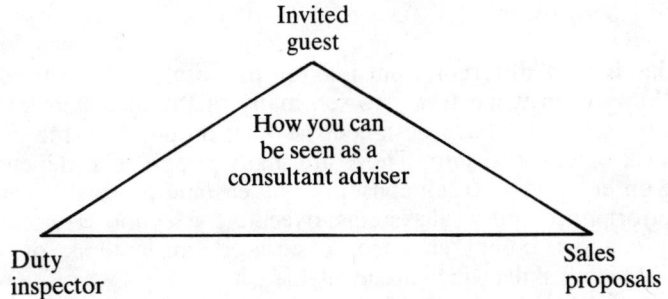

Invitations

I am fortunate to have been invited by many organizations to work on a wide variety of problems. They range between working on a city government problem in one of the Canadian provinces, developing teamwork amongst commercial airline pilots in Australia, resolving conflicts in a chemical company in England and facilitating the development of managers in a US bank. In addition, I have had a chance to advise manufacturing, petroleum and engineering companies, telecommunications and travel enterprises, advertising agencies, insurance organizations, retailers, breweries, coal companies and professional practices and institutes. Each of these assignments has been an integral part of my own personal development.

How did I come to be invited in the first instance? When I look back on the wide range of organizations which have asked me to contribute to their work, I find that there are four basic ways in which I came to be invited. People heard me speak at a conference, they read one of my papers or books, they attended a course at which I was teaching or they were referred by other people. Virtually all of the invitations have come through personal contact.

However, an invitation is not a contract. It is initially an opportunity to meet with other people and discuss the issues in order to decide if there is sufficient ground upon which to proceed. This means assessing myself as the consultant adviser, in terms of what I can contribute. An invitation is an opportunity to talk with other people, on their own territory, about issues which they regard as important. As a guest, it is important to say, but not at length, who you are and what you have done.

The important point to remember is that you are a guest, and must listen intently to what other people have to say. If they trust you, they will give the appropriate cues and it is the extent to which you build on these cues that you will be judged. If you miss the cues you might not be invited again. If, however, you pick them up quickly and encourage the clients to talk further, often between themselves for the first time, then you may not only be invited again, but be given a contract.

Making proposals

All this is very different from making proposals. I have used the 'proposal' approach when trying to sell many of the management education programmes that I have designed. Making proposals is the most important task of salesmanship. There are many people who depend for their living on being able to sell consultancy ideas and processes, whether they be performance appraisal systems, executive selection services, wage and salary systems, computer software services and systems, or any of the other advisory skills which are available.

The person who is involved in making proposals as a consultant adviser is essentially a solution-centred consultant. That is, he or she has a solution and goes in search of problems to which it might be applied. However, when he does not find a problem, there may still be the necessity to sell, and solution proposals can be put forward for problems which don't exist.

Making proposals is a hard life. One must expect many rejections. The sales person involved in making consultancy advisory proposals is more likely to get no's rather than yes's. It takes courage, conviction and a determined belief in the services that one is selling, in order to keep going.

Doing your inspection duty

The third main form of consultancy advisory work is when you are called upon to do your duty. In many ways, sitting on an appointing committee is a duty. This is particularly so in formal organizations where a certain number of people have to serve on the board so that an official appointment can be made. Very often you are not directly involved in the department in which the person will work, yet, in order to ensure that the proper processes are adhered to, you may be asked to take part in the interview selection process. I have found that in this role I am upholding the rules and procedures of the organization.

People in the auditing and accounting profession often find themselves in the role of a consultant adviser, imposing a duty upon clients. In effect, they are required by law to go through certain processes and report their findings. Therefore clients regard them more as duty inspectors rather than as consultant advisers.

Overview

Of the three main approaches to consulting where do you find most of your work falls? Are you in the position of being an invited guest, or a salesperson or a duty inspector? In most cases we have all three aspects in varying degrees. But the proportion may not be the way you want it. So

- What balance in your consulting advisory work are you looking for?
- What strategies do you have for moving to achieve that balance?

How do you see your role?

Gaining an assignment is one thing, but the role you play is dependent more on your own style and the relationship you have with your clients. There are three broad roles that you can play as a consultant adviser. You need to be aware of each one so that you do not end up in the wrong role.

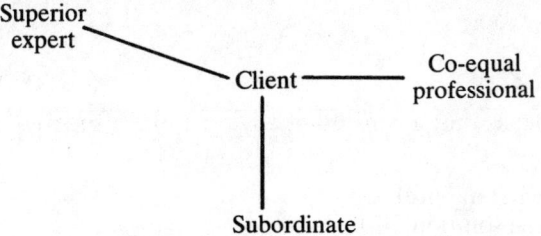

Over time you will have the opportunity to perform in all three of these roles. Each one emerges during the interaction that takes place in the consulting relationship. Let us look at some quick examples.

Jim Nelson was a work study adviser with a manufacturing company. He was sitting in his office when he received the following call from the manufacturing manager Bob Rowton:

Rowton: I want you to come over and look at the speed on the packing conveyor.
Nelson: What's wrong?
Rowton: I don't know. The operatives say it's going too fast. They are threatening to stop work.
Nelson: We tested it last week and it was going at the right speed.
Rowton: Well, I want you to test it again.
Nelson: Maybe the speed is not really the problem.
Rowton: Look, just test the speed so we can get these people back to work.

Clearly Rowton is under pressure and he starts to treat Nelson, who does not report to him, like a subordinate. Should Nelson accept this or seek to change the role relationship? It may well be that Nelson sees himself as the person who knows most about the system and feels he should behave as a superior expert. If so he might say, 'Look, I know what I'm talking about. The speed was calculated according to the standard systems and procedures. There is no point in doing it again.'

Alternatively, Nelson can try to change the relationship to a problem solving co-equal partner by saying, 'I appreciate you want to get the people back on the job but it would be the best use of my time if you and I met first to talk over the problem, before we do another test.'

Now, in these case examples, Nelson does not use the words 'superior expert' or 'co-equal professional', but indicates clearly the relationship he wants. If the client rejects this then Nelson has to decide whether he can continue working in such a role.

Many consultant advisers feel they have little choice in the role they play. If they are internal advisers they may feel that the status of the client in the organization hierarchy determines their role. If they are external advisers they may feel that to retain the job they have to fit in with the role definition given by the client.

My view is that there is a time and a place for all three roles but it should be related to the task, not the status of the people involved.

'Superior expert' role

For example, I want a consultant adviser to be a superior expert when he or she:

- knows what the problem is,
- knows the solution,

- is technically competent, and
- has my agreement to act as a superior expert.

Now these conditions usually apply when I go to the dentist, the optician, the doctor or an electrician or plumber. Once I have confidence that they know the problem and can provide a technically competent answer, I do not mind receiving advice from a superior expert (providing, of course, they don't deal with me in a condescending way).

'Subordinate' role

Equally, I believe there is a time for consultant advisers to be subordinate in their role when:

- the client knows the problem,
- the adviser has a solution that does not require in-depth discussion, and
- the solution can be implemented without further consultation.

'Co-equal professional' role

However, most of the time I find the co-equal professional role the one that suits me and others as consultant advisers best. Here I work with a client to identify and diagnose the problem or opportunity, then gather and discuss data to effect improvements.

In such a relationship there is a mutual respect for each other's skills and knowledge. I see my role as a partner in problem solving, rather than instructing someone as a superior expert or fulfilling someone else's instructions as a subordinate.

It is important that you identify the role you wish to have and work to establish that rather than letting the role be determined solely by the client. My experience is that the most favourable situation is when you are an 'invited guest' and working in a co-equal professional role. However, this is not always possible.

Consider the assignments you have had and reflect on the relationships that have governed the work you have done. Each one of them will have had aspects of the various roles that have been described.

Improving organization renewal

Gordon Lippitt provided an example of how to consult through his many writings and his educational work. He was a personality – a big man with big ideas and a belief that problems could be resolved.

His commitment was to what he termed Organization Renewal, and he wrote an influential book with that title. He saw organization renewal emerging through managers being skilled in building and managing effective teams. He particularly highlighted the training profession as having an important role to play in this as facilitators rather than teachers.

He edited a special issue of the *Journal of European Training* in 1975 on 'The Role of the Training Director as an Internal Consultant'. He emphasized the need for problem solving consultation via four main paths.

1   It should be task-oriented, not self-oriented. By this he meant the goal was to improve the way the task was done rather than to gain credit for individuals.
2   The processes should be collaborative and involve those affected by the change.
3   The methods of problem solving should be experimental, where people are encouraged to try out new approaches through mutual agreement.
4   The methods should be educational, helping people grow as individuals and be better able to resolve future problems.

He was helpful to others with words of wisdom based on case example. He was also a creator of educational simulations through which one could assess one's own practice. He also emphasized the importance of having a code of ethics to guide consultative practice.

It is useful perhaps to conclude by listing the points Lippitt suggested we concentrate upon if we are to be better at consulting.

'(a)   Focus on the problem-solving approach to learning and change: use data, not just hunches.
(b)   Develop interdependence with others, not dependency.
(c)   Practise what we preach in the field of our specialized knowledges.
(d)   Diagnose situations, rather than merely treat symptoms.
(e)   Understand ourselves so thoroughly that we do not let our personal needs get in the way of helping people and organizations to develop.
(f)   Communicate on a reality level in "open" fashion.
(g)   Admit mistakes and learn from failure.
(h)   Develop interests and skills so as to be able to work with people in a controlling manner.
(i)   Be willing to experiment and innovate.
(j)   Develop personal philosophy about working and developing people and organizations.
(k)   Be capable of saying, "I don't know."
(l)   Be willing to learn and change.

These criteria may not be the most important or only criteria for professional behaviour, but they are some I value highly. Unfortunately, I find I am unable to achieve these standards as consistently as I wish.' Lippitt 1975.

Ethics of accepting or rejecting assignments

What we say and do is what we are. Our values are reflected in our behaviour. Accepting or rejecting assignments is an important decision. Under what conditions should you say 'no' and thereby reject an assignment? Clearly, when the task lies outside your own field of competence or conflicts with other priorities. However, there are other situations which require careful consideration. In this section there are examples of some consulting and advisory tasks which I have rejected.

I like being invited to work on projects, but there are occasions when I have to say 'no'. All consultant advisers will be confronted with situations where they have to question whether they should contribute to a particular project. It is important that one has some values to guide one's decisions in advance.

I have outlined four occasions on which I can remember having said 'no' when asked to be involved in a project. On each occasion the reason for saying 'no' was different. In summarizing each of these particular incidents you may wish to consider how you would have acted in similar circumstances.

No involvement

The first consultancy project which I refused came after I had written an article in a national newspaper about wage systems and industrial relations. I received a telephone call from the managing director of a medium-sized organization, who asked me to meet with him to discuss particular problems he had within his organization. He said that he had liked my article, as it related exactly to a problem in his own organization. He wanted my advice on how to resolve differences between different wage rates which were causing industrial relations problems.

The meeting did not start well. I told him that it would be important for me to talk with those people who were concerned about the issues, in order to gain a full understanding of the problem. He said that he did not want anyone talking to his staff and he asked me directly what methods and techniques I had that could help with the problem. I replied that, until I understood the problem, it was impossible for me to make any suggestions.

We had a rather circular conversation for about half an hour. He was pressing me for specific solutions and I was seeking to further understand the problem. As I perceived it, I was seeking to be problem-centred and he was seeking to be solution-centred. As far as he was concerned, he knew what the problem was and he now wanted my technical expertise, in order to solve it in the way that you would call an electrician when you wanted the lights fixed, or a plumber when you wanted the taps to stop dripping.

I eventually told him that I could not work in the way he was suggesting. I therefore concluded the meeting and said that I felt he should look for someone else who would be more in line with his approach to the job. I was not prepared to offer solutions until I had a wider understanding of the problem, which meant involving others in the discussion. We parted, and that was the end of a project which never really began.

Conflict of values

The second project which I felt unable to participate in was an invitation from an international company that was manufacturing cigarettes. I have never been attracted to smoking, and have always felt that it is a health hazard, especially since research has suggested that there is a relationship between smoking and lung cancer. In this case I was asked to work on an organization programme concerning the work design and staff motivation in a new factory.

I felt it would be contravening my principles to advise on this project. Although my contribution would have been a small one in the wider context of the organization, I thought would be inappropriate to support the further development of a product with which I disagreed. I explained this to the two representatives of the organization. They said they understood, and our discussion came to a halt. Needless to say, I have not been invited by them to work on any subsequent projects in other parts of the organization that do not produce cigarettes.

I should say, however, that I have worked for companies that do produce cigarettes, but not in the specific division concerned with that particular product. I have contributed to the general management education programmes of organizations which, amongst other products, have produced cigarettes. Of course the question is, where does one draw the line? Many multinational companies produce products which we disfavour. For my part, I have only refused to work on assignments which are specifically concerned with the production of the actual product of which I disapprove.

Overlapping roles

A third case arose when I was invited to work with a public service organization. I was asked to help facilitate a meeting of the internal staff with a person who was employed as an outside educational designer.

I had a number of meetings with the civil servants and the outside designer. However, after discussing the issues with them both, I felt that my intervention, rather than helping, would merely get in the way, and duplicate the efforts of the other consultant. I said this to them both and they agreed with my conclusion. Although I was depriving myself of what could have been an interesting assignment, I felt it was right to tell the people that, in this particular case, I could make no significant contribution additional to that of the educational designer.

Role overload

The fourth example also occurred with a public service organization. In this case, I had been working on a project and built up a good relationship with the internal staff member. Up until the point when I had to withdraw,

I had been involved in serious discussions with senior managers regarding the direction of the organization and, in particular, the training and development to be given to senior management. Through various discussions and trial programmes, we had developed a successful workshop in the area of teamwork. My feeling was that I had made my contribution in the diagnosis, and the development and design of the workshop.

However, the internal staff member felt it was essential that I continue to contribute in a tutoring role. Because of other commitments, I said that this would not be possible, due to the amount of time involved. I suggested that one of my colleagues, who was equally knowledgeable in the area, could deal with at least half of the assignment. This proposal was not acceptable to the internal staff member. I therefore had to say that it would be impossible for me to continue with the assignment, and we parted company. I felt in this situation that I was under excessive pressure to give up too much of my time to the project. In essence, I felt that the client was becoming too dependent and too demanding on me.

How much choice do you have?

All of the above examples illustrate situations where I have felt it would have been inappropriate to continue. In your own consultancy advisory work you will find similar situations. You may feel that in the cases I have described you would have continued, or perhaps even taken a different approach to the client.

I recognize it is easier to say 'no' when you are an external consultant. It is not so easy when you are a member of the organization and consulting with senior people who can perhaps have an influence on your career. In the above examples, I was an external consultant in every case. I felt, therefore, relatively free to make the choices that I made. However, if I had been destitute and my wife and family had had no roof over their heads, then perhaps I would have thought again about saying 'no'. I readily acknowledge that we can all be clear on our principles when we are not under pressure. However, when things get difficult, we may have to reassess how often and when we say 'no'. The important question is, what are the principles which guide our actions in saying either 'yes' or 'no'?

Guidelines

This chapter has covered some of the chief role issues affecting the consulting advisory relationship. How you are seen and the way you respond can determine the outcome of the work assignment.

You need to have a model of how to advise. I see my role as a co-equal problem solver helping clients on a journey. My contribution is to help them think out their destination and gain some help with the vehicles and maps. In that sense I have a travel agent image of my work. While this may not at first seem appealing, it does deal with many of the issues.

In order to apply the models, consider your last assignment and assess what relationships you held during the task and how it influenced the performance of your work.

Establishing the appropriate role relationship is critical to success in consulting work and the principles identified in this chapter provide a base upon which you can assess where you are and to develop the relevant role relationships.

Exercise

1   Provide examples in each box of matrix if possible of assignments you have had.

	Co-equal professional	Subordinate	Superior expert
Invited guest			
Sales person			
Inspection agent			

2   What do you think are the principal role relationships that the following normally have to face in their work, based on the above model? You can use the numbers in the matrix to signify the main relationships. It may be that a person plays more than one role during the assignment.
(a)   Internal auditors
(b)   External auditors
(c)   Safety advisers
(d)   Tax accountants
(e)   Architects
(f)   Management consultants
(g)   Dentists
(h)   Quantity surveyors
(i)   Travel consultants
(j)   Quality controllers
(k)   Computer advisers
(l)   Your role
(m)   Others

3   What are the principles that govern whether you accept or reject an assignment?

4   What assignments have you rejected and why?

10 How managers can consult

'One gives nothing so freely as advice'

La Rochefoucauld, *Les Maximes*

Sharing managerial experience

Managers can help each other in many ways by taking on an advisory role and improving the workplace by comparing problems and sharing solutions. Managing laterally is as important as managing hierarchically. However, to do so one needs to have effective consultant adviser skills.

I have always been surprised how few people of the same level in an organization see each other perform the same job. People in leadership positions can be of considerable help to each other as advisers if they are given the opportunity. Here are some examples where I have enabled managers to act as consultants to each other.

Airline captains

I was asked to design and deliver a team management programme for airline captains and their crew (Margerison, Davies and McCann 1987). I asked the captains how often they had the opportunity to see another captain work. To my surprise they said that once they had qualified as a captain they rarely, if ever, saw any other captain fly an aircraft. They obviously had the opportunity to see a first officer fly an aircraft under their command but never had the chance to compare themselves to someone of their own experience and learn from them.

Together with my colleagues we designed an experimental workshop where the pilots and flight engineers could explore team work issues. This included 'swapping' jobs in role play situations, as well as behavioural modelling examples.

Manufacturing managers

In another organization I was asked to work with the top team to see how they could improve their performance. It was felt that the main departments did not cooperate or understand each other's functions well enough.

The discussion had been going for nearly two hours and the manufacturing manager had said very little. Suddenly he leant forward in his chair. 'I've been thinking about the way our departments work and it is a reflection of the way we work. We have agreed this morning we must be more customer and market-orientated, but I've worked for over twenty years in manufacturing. In that time I've never met a customer; I've not gone looking for them and no one has introduced them to me.' There was a silence in the meeting. The point was understood. There was a need for a closer comparing and sharing between the departments. The managers began then to discuss how they could consult and advise each other and set the example for their departments.

Tourist managers

Likewise, when consulting with a large tourist company I had the opportunity to meet with managers who were in charge of various regions. We had managers from the major cities in Europe at the workshop. It seemed to me that they had very similar problems of managing their resorts.

There were the inevitable problems of finding enough beds for the visitors, negotiating with the hoteliers, ensuring that the relationships with the coach companies and the airlines were in order and other problems including industrial relations through to financial and medical issues. In all it was a complex set of managerial problems which each one of them confronted.

During the workshop, which was designed to try to improve the overall management of the resorts, I asked the managers how often they had the opportunity to visit each other's area and learn from their colleagues. Again, to my surprise, I found that they never visited each other's territories. The only chance they had to compare notes was at management meetings or an annual conference. However, the managerial meetings were always crowded with other business matters and the conference never really addressed the issue of how they could learn from each other.

Managerial consultation by action leading

The work of Professor Reg Revans (1982) stands out as a brilliant example of how to design a mutual advisory and consulting group to improve individual and organizational performance. On the surface his ideas look so obvious and simple that anyone could and should be able to implement them.

In so many organizations there is a vast amount of learning that can take place through the structured sharing of experience. This has become established largely through Action Learning programmes. The idea was originally launched by Professor Reg Revans when working at the National Coal Board in England after the Second World War. He refers to it as the 'Comrades in Adversity' approach.

Revans has said that those who act as consultant advisers in an action learning enterprise should 'set out to contrive the conditions in which managers may learn, with and from each other, how to manage better in the course of their daily tasks'.

Straightforward, but it requires real consultative skill, as I have found from my own efforts to get managers to learn with and from each other on real life cases rather than hypothetical standard cases. You see, in the real world, things won't stand still while you study them.

He introduced the scheme whereby managers in one colliery could go and visit another colliery with the direct objective of learning how others did things. It was no use just talking about it. The managers actually had to go and observe what was happening at the other collieries and to see to what extent the ideas could be applied in their own colliery.

He has subsequently used the action learning approach with success in a wide variety of situations. These include bringing together doctors, nurses and administrators in ten London hospitals to work together on joint problems; bringing managers together from different parts of the same organization, as he did in the GEC in the UK; working in Belgium to bring people from different organizations together, such as bankers moving to engineering organizations and engineers to banks. These together with other initiatives in Africa, Asia, North America and Australasia have shown how action learning is a powerful vehicle to enable managers to consult and learn from each other. Now the International Management Centre under the leadership of Professor Gordon Wills (Wills 1984), has established a business school on the Action Learning principles and enables managers to qualify for a Master of Business Administration and other qualifications by Action Learning. The philosophy and example of Revan's work has been tested and found valid. Managers can consult and learn from each other. Indeed the laboratory of real work must be the starting point.

The action learning approach enables set advisers (not experts) to guide and coach managers to resolve problems through mutual collaboration. There are four main ways in which this can be done.

Consulting methods for managers

		Situation	
		Familiar	Unfamiliar
Task	Familiar	Own job same situation	Own job new situation
	Unfamiliar	New job same situation	New job new situation

In each case the manager has a project and meets with other managers who have projects. They meet in a set and learn by doing and passing on what they learn and how they learnt it.

Action learning is a powerful form of consultation. It involves managers consulting with and for each other. They take their recommendations more seriously than those proposed by external consultants, for they have diagnosed, analysed and developed the options themselves. It does, however, require skilled facilitators to set it up and guide it to provide enough structure to ensure progress without interfering so much that it takes over the task from the managers. Managers can be very effective as consultant advisers and become their own change agents if they have sufficient confidence and the right action learning system.

There is a community and a system governing the action learning relationships as shown below.

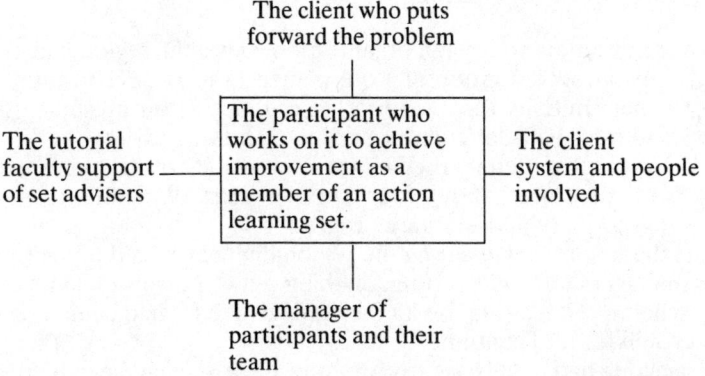

It sounds a rather obvious approach to improving managerial practice. However, I still find in my own consultancy and advisory work that there is relatively little crossing of organizational boundaries by managers on an organized learning basis. If people go to other people's offices or factories or coalmines it is for a specific meeting or task.

Interchange schemes

I support the notion of setting up consultancy arrangements between managers. That is, I believe it is useful if a manager can enter into a 'share and compare' relationship with another colleague who is doing a similar job, in order to interchange on a regular basis. If, for example, Manager A who is in charge of an organization in one area agrees to meet with another manager in another area to share and compare notes over a period of a year, then this is likely to have some important consequences.

For example, if you are the manager of factory X, and you know you are going to get a visit from the manager of factory Z, then you will try your hardest to have your organization looking its best. You will put some effort into thinking of ways of improving performance. You will not want your place to look deficient and ineffective when your colleague visits. Likewise, if he is coming with the purpose of learning how you do things then it is probable he would be open to sharing what he had done and taking some pride in discussing it.

Likewise, if the manager of factory Z knows that a couple of months later you will be making a return visit, then he or she will do their best to ensure that things are in good order and ideas to effect improvement have taken place. This is particularly so if it is understood that the aim of the visits is to share and compare and learn so that both of you can introduce ideas into your organization that have been applied elsewhere. Here a mutual learning can take place. However, the atmosphere has to be right. It has to be agreed that the managers are in fact acting as consultants to each other.

The inter-store consulting project

I was a consultant to a retail organization where the regional manager and I encouraged a group of store managers to act as consultants to each other. Initially they were rather sceptical. I set up some guidelines and ran a half-day training session on how to advise.

The managers then worked in duos and made arrangements to visit each other's stores about four times a year. We built in review meetings to share and compare progress.

At the first review meeting the regional manager said to me that, if the managers were not getting anything out of it, we should abandon the scheme. To his surprise all the managers felt it had been a success and voted for it to continue.

Each one had a real case study of how he or she had been helped by colleagues. The interchange had also strengthened team cooperation and morale. It was a classic example of how managers can consult each other and make an impact. An additional benefit in this case was that other managers below store manager level had become involved and it had generated their enthusiasm and commitment.

Reciprocal consulting

I believe that managers can act as consultant advisers to each other and do so very productively. Indeed one of the most powerful functions of the good manager is to help others learn from his or her experience. I do, however, believe that we neglect this great opportunity for people to develop their performance.

I would like to see more programmes where managers become consultant advisers on a joint and reciprocal basis with colleagues who have similar problems. I believe this could be done concurrently with the job they have. All it needs is a structure within which it can work and the support of top management.

I prefer to see a half-yearly or annual conference where managers have to report back on what they have been doing by way of working with at least one other colleague on a consultant advisory basis. They could report back on how they have worked with each other and what particular areas they have been able to develop. In this way managers can become consultant advisers and consultant advisers can become better managers. All senior managers should attend these presentations and make it their job to ensure the best ideas for improvement are introduced in other parts of the organization. I feel this may reduce the need for consultant advisers from outside the organization, while ensuring that improvements do occur.

Mixed group consulting

Another classic example of how managers can profitably consult with each other is the Business Management Programme at the ACI Company in Melbourne, Australia. I worked with the Director of Human Resources, Barry Smith, to establish an innovative top management programme for many of the top 400 managers in this conglomerate organization that has over 20,000 employees worldwide.

It was decided the best way to develop top managers was to give them real organization projects of strategic significance. These included:

- how we develop an export strategy and apply it for a major timber product
- how we establish an occupational health and safety scheme that works throughout the organization
- how we manage the human resource issues in acquisitions and disbursements.
- how to reorganize a manufacturing operation by integrating plants from different geographical areas on to one site.

These projects plus many others formed the basis upon which managers worked together in groups of three to five over two or three months. The groups were composed in the main of people who were not 'experts' in the field under study. Their job was to learn and advise. We had people like the corporate lawyer and the manager of glass manufacture working together on areas outside their normal work. However, they had to continue with their normal job at the same time.

The results have been an outstanding success. Managers have not only learnt from each other, but also contributed significantly to business development. By having to ask naive questions in areas in which they were not knowledgeable they not only found how businesses were run, but got people to think of new ways of doing things.

Consulting to line managers

The role of the consultant adviser varies not only between functions but also between organizations. Some organizations use their consultant advisers as controllers, others use them as explorers and developers.

Internal consulting at ITT

A good example of both roles can be seen in the organization structure set up by Harold Geneen, the legendary president and chief executive officer of the International Telephone and Telegraph Company. He established an internal consulting and advisory staff at headquarters who, according to Geneen, 'could go anywhere in the company and ask any kind of questions and get any kind of answers and he could report his findings to my office. These staff men out of headquarters cut through the structured rigidity of the formal organization, monitoring each of the subsidiaries. The accounting staff man monitored the profits, the engineering staff monitored the engineering department, and so on, with marketing, personnel and legal . . . In addition to this regular staff we had at the time twelve to sixteen senior staff men designated as product line managers. Each of them roamed over the complete product lines representing the competition. The product line managers succeeded only by persuading our line managers that they were not out to get them personally, that they were there to help them!' (Geneen and Moscow 1984).

Geneen outlines in some detail the proactive role he saw the product line managers playing in the ITT system. 'The product line managers were free of the responsibilities of budgets and performance. They had in effect a licence to speculate on what could be done differently and better. They were free to be imaginative and creative. All they had to do was to sell their ideas to the line managers and work with them for the improvement of the company. If they could not agree, once again the difference in opinion would be reported, aired and settled at the headquarters level.'

Changing roles

Therefore Geneen deliberately built into his organization roles for people who would act in a controlling way and those who would explore and advise in a creative way. It may well be that the distinction between these two approaches to consulting is beginning to change and begin to develop into a continuum along which consultants move.

For example, the internal auditor's role has traditionally been that of a controller inspector looking for variances on a 'check and tick' system and asking for explanations when variances occurred. This role still continues, but today internal auditors are extending their traditional role to be proactive in consulting on organizational improvements, particularly those in the area of effectiveness or efficiency.

Such work therefore involves the internal auditor working in a proactive way with managers rather than just as an inspector. From time to time the role conflict may occur when the controller inspector and the creator innovator roles cross each other. It is sometimes difficult to be seen by clients as a free-thinking creator innovator when they also know you as a person who is concerned with checking detail variations.

How managers consult each day

Consulting and counselling are now a large part of a manager's daily activity. This is a developing aspect of the managerial role and covers a wide range of activities.

Performance review: Most organizations have introduced some system of assessing and improving staff performance. It is the manager's job to do this in a planned professional way. You can be seen as either a 'critical judge' or a 'helpful adviser'. The manager with good consulting skills will be able to set up a meeting based on understanding in order to help staff members improve their own performance. The 'helpful adviser' role will come first and the 'critical judge' will usually be the agent of last resort.

Career counselling: Making the right choice in job selection is now widely recognized as of importance to both the individual and the organization. Line managers, rather than personnel people, have a crucial role in facilitating such discussions with staff and finding out their views and options. This is a vital consultative role where the experience of the senior manager can aid the other staff member.

Personal counselling: Increasingly managers find that employees bring personal and domestic worries and problems to them. Where this happens, the manager is being asked to act as a consultant. By listening and advising in a considerate way the manager can often make a contribution. Consulting skills are therefore important in dealing with such matters.

Work problem solving: Very often a manager has to act as a consultant in his or her own work team. There may be differences of opinion where neither person is right. The manager here can act as a catalyst to get those involved to discuss things in depth and come to an agreement.

Individual job advice: As a manager you will from time to time be asked by individual members of your team for your views rather than your decision. They will expect you to act as a consultant based on your wider understanding of the job. Here there is always a thin line between taking control and making the decision, and simply giving advice and letting others make the decision.

Representative advice: The manager represents the team in various meetings. There they have to give and receive advice and in doing so are part of the consultative process.

Upward advice: At various times your own boss will ask for your views more as a consultant than a line manager. On such occasions you need to consider whether you raise questions or give answers or both.

Joint development activities: Professor John Morris (Morris and Burgoyne 1975) of the Manchester Business School in the UK has been a leading proponent of managers improving performance by consultative processes. His approach has involved teams of managers working on problems in association with academics from the business school.

This structure has had numerous successes. The value lies in the outside support that is available to managers to gain the added knowledge and skills they require to solve the issues. However, as Morris has stressed, the central important item is the meeting of managers to provide each other with the benefits of their experience.

Overview: These are just some examples of how managers increasingly have to act as consultants as a normal part of their everyday job. The map shows the main elements and how your job relates to giving and receiving consultative advice.

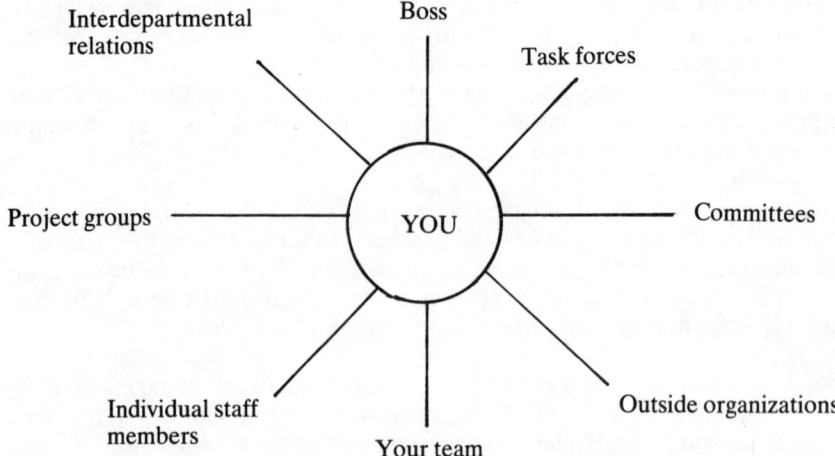

Guidelines

Today it is increasingly difficult to separate out our advisory or consulting work from our executive managerial work. The demands of the job are such that we have to cross boundaries both within and without the organization to influence others if we are to be successful in our jobs. Consulting skills are an integral aspect of work, rather than something tacked on at the end. An effective manager is in essence increasingly an effective consultant.

Consulting advisory skills are applicable at all levels of management. Indeed the higher a person goes in management the more likely they are to be involved in consulting assignments not only in their own organization but also for outside bodies such as professional institutes, government departments, educational organizations and other bodies. There is also the need to advise and consult with a wide range of people in your own organization.

Exercise

1   Consider your job and assess what consulting roles you have against the following list.

Internal

- Committees
- Task forces
- Project groups
- Interdepartmental relations
- Workshops

External

- Professional institutes
- Government departments
- Educational organizations
- Seminars
- Others

2   Today all consultants have to manage and all managers have to consult. The only difference is the relative priority and time allocation given to each. The principles outlined here can be as valid for managers as they are for consultants. What percentage of time do you allocate to both areas?

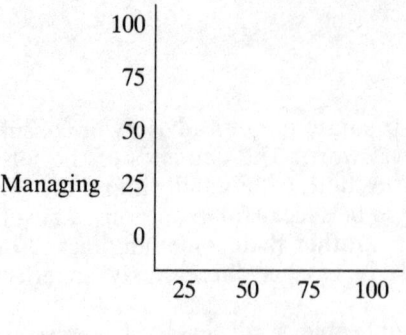

Consulting

3   Based on the above model how do you spend your time at work? What changes, if any, need to be made in your time allocation?

11 What is your systems overview?

'Ah love! Could thou and I with Fate conspire to grasp this sorry Scheme of Things entire would not we shatter it to bits – and then re-mould it nearer to the Heart's Desire!'

Rubaiyat of Omar Khayyám, transl. Edward Fitzgerald

The organization as a system

Solving organizational problems is difficult because so many people and parts of an organization are involved. There is rarely one answer or one person who can solve the problem. Often an improvement in one area of the organization can lead to failure in another. That is why it is important for a consultant adviser to have a systems overview. That is, you need an understanding of all the people, organizations and internal and external aspects of the system with which you are working. This is often called open systems consulting.

I believe that the consultant adviser is primarily an action researcher. His or her job is to 'work with members of the organization, to identify the features that they feel are impeding their effectiveness, and to help them to gather data, which they can use to resolve difficulties. In these processes, the adviser may use a wide variety of psychological, sociological, anthropological and other behavioural science methods and ideas in his work.

This means getting to grips with the organizational system. In the past, and even today, consultant advisers have been accused of pushing their solution, their package, their particular potion, regardless of whether it fitted the organizational system. The rise of the contingency schools of organizational behaviour theorists challenged the general applicability of such packages. The need to look at the way different cultures affected techniques and methods has been stressed. The importance of the 'open systems' approach has been clearly demonstrated.

The paint-spraying case

One of my favourite examples of the need for the open systems approach comes from a case originally put forward by Anselm Strauss and Alex Bavelas (1955) and subsequently written up as the Hovey Beard case. It is

129

a classic of how success leads to failure because Bavelas, the consultant, and the manager did not take an open systems view.

The company manufactured wooden toys. The toys were cut in an assembly shop and then sent to the painting department. The painting was done by women who had to work to a specific schedule set by the timing of a conveyor system. The belt took the dolls they painted into a kiln. The system, introduced as a result of work study, replaced the old approach in which the women worked at their own pace.

The Production System

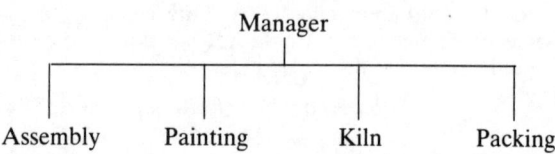

| Assembly | Painting | Kiln | Packing |

By the end of the second month of the new system, many of the conveyor hooks were going into the kiln empty. Unpainted toys were piling up in the paint shop, and at the other end the packaging department had less and less to do.

The women protested that they were not going to work under these new conditions. As production was suffering, the manager invited a consultant in and discussions took place on the cause of the problem. Poor ventilation and the pace of the conveyor belt emerged as important issues. The women proposed: 'Let us adjust the speed of the belt faster or slower depending on how we feel.' The management were suspicious of this, but let the proposal go ahead for a trial period. Overall output increased to the extent that within three weeks the women were operating at 30 to 50 percent above the level that had been expected under the original arrangement.

However, this success had not taken account of the effects on the wider system – namely the assembly and the packing departments. Suddenly they were under pressure to produce and service more toys. No one had consulted them about this. Now instead of having a fixed work schedule they had 'peak' load pressures, depending on when the women decided to increase the speed of the conveyor.

The complaints from the men in these other departments reached the manager. He decided that there was a need for a standard pace and re-established the system introduced by the work study people. The result was that the painting foreman, and many of the women, left.

This classic case shows the importance of identifying the system you are trying to change. The manager and the consultant concentrated on the paint department at the expense of the other departments. Yet the solution they arrived at for the trial period affected the men in assembly and packing. A narrow definition of the system led to an intervention that succeeded in one area, but caused failure in the wider system. Moreover, the manager and the consultant had not taken into account the different cultures in each department.

It is easy to see with hindsight what perhaps could have been done. Certainly more consultation, but with whom? Should the three departments have been brought together? Should the foremen have met? Should the union representative have been involved? All of these vital questions concerning the management of the change process. The answers depend on the nature of the political and work systems.

Identifying forces in the system

Much of the early work in diagnosing the open systems approach was done by Kurt Lewin (1963) in his classic work on field theory. It still bears in-depth study today and I have found his ideas useful. The force field analysis method is one easy way to start looking at the open systems issues. The simplified force field analysis chart, as shown below, can be helpful in getting people to verbalize and visualize the issues.

Force field analysis

Forces which will help the change process	Forces which will hinder the change process
a	x
b	y
c	z

In the Hovey Beard case, this form of analysis would probably have brought to the surface the system problems. Is this approach relevant to the work you are doing? What are the factors in the wider organizational system that will help or hinder success?

This case illustrates the way all consultant advisers must, as stressed earlier, be aware of territories. If you exercise influence and change something in one area it usually has an impact on another area. While the girls in the paint shop wanted to go at their own pace, this upset the regular schedules that had been accepted in the other departments. Therefore, consider the way your consultancy advice will affect people in different territories. To what extent do you need to involve people from outside the immediate area in which you have been asked to advise and consult?

The concept of organizational territory is central to any consulting activity. You are by the nature of your task invariably working on or with someone else's territory. You will be working in an office or a unit or a division in which a manager sees himself or herself accountable for what takes place. You require permission not only to enter this territory but to work there. Likewise when you see problems, as in the above case, between departments you need to find ways of facilitating problem solving discussions between people from different territories and gain their permission to intervene.

Consulting models in practice

The best selling book *In Search of Excellence* by Tom Peters and Robert Waterman (1982) gave them instant fame and prominence as consultant advisers. However, like most people who gain instant fame, they had been working at it for a few years.

They had previously written an article in *Business Horizons* in 1980 called 'Structure Is Not Organization', which has become something of a classic and reflects an integrated approach to consulting.

They identified a number of factors which need to be integrated if organizations are to improve. They called this the 7S Model as shown below.

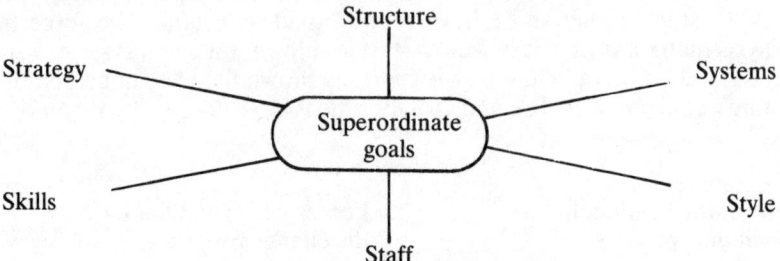

The value of this model is that it highlights the need for all consultant advisers to be aware that changing one factor is likely to affect other aspects of the organization. This is often called the 'contingency approach' in that one thing depends on another.

An earlier version of this kind of systems thinking was developed by Professor Hal Leavitt (1965), who said all organizational change has to take into account the interdependencies of the following

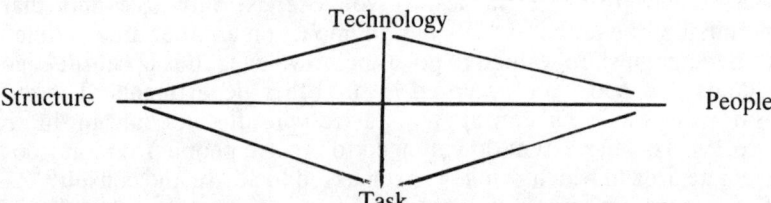

Now these models do not tell us how to consult, but they do indicate what to look for. If you change the way a task is done what will that do to the people, their skills, their role structure and so on? To be a good consultant it is vital to have a map in your mind of the implications so you can get ahead of the game and read the likely moves. This is what we normally call anticipation, and combined with experience is one of the most important aspects in the design and management of consulting assignment.

Recognizing the system network

The question is, how do you go about helping clients to manage a change that goes beyond any particular unit or system? The first step requires that you start to visualize the data you receive as a network of contacts and influences. As the client describes the actors, their scripts and the plot, listen carefully to how the overall system works. You will find it is a network of contacts.

The client is usually under some form of pressure to do things within a period of time. Very often the client has not thought through how to cope or respond in a proactive way to these pressures. I have spent hours working with clients to help them see their personal network of contacts and influences so they can work out a strategy and range of priorities. This is another aspect of understanding and working with a systems framework. However, when I am working with clients on such matters I refer to their personal action network.

At the centre of every consulting assignment there is a person or people who have to do something, usually with others, in order to improve the situation that faces them. They have a network of people whom they need to influence. Alternatively others will seek to put pressure on your client to influence him or her.

Draw out the key pressures

It takes time to discover these pressures and one has to be patient. People will not always tell you who is putting pressure on them. Your task is to develop an understanding of their network and the way it affects the problem solving process.

A good example is shown in the following case. Phil Adams was a chemist. He was offered the position of management development manager because he knew most people in the organization and he wanted a wider role in his last ten years with the company, rather than just being the chief chemist.

He took the job and soon found many problems. The old seniority system for promotion was breaking down. Young professional staff were not prepared to be time servers waiting for 'dead men's shoes'. Too many of the better young professionals were leaving for opportunities elsewhere.

Phil Adams was given the task of coming up with proposals for managing professional and managerial staff based on performance, and developing the appropriate people for higher management. Phil had proved himself an excellent researcher and competent administrator. Now, he realized, he had to 'run quickly to stand still'. He sought advice on how to tackle the problem.

My first reaction was to find out where he stood in his system. What was the network of people and roles that surrounded him? The reason I took this approach was to find out the pressures that he would have to satisfy if he was to make progress. As he talked, it became obvious that the network of pressure was considerable. Some of his comments were: 'The engineers are not content to wait for the company to do something. Many of them are taking external qualifications in management ... The administrative people have made a stand on the seniority issue and it is difficult to promote people in those areas on the basis of performance ... Our appraisal system is not adequate for assessing the performance of one person compared to another. Many of our managers ignore it ... Our managing director is very keen on an assessment centre and wants to introduce this system ... We send two or three senior people each year to these long eight-week management courses, but I don't think they are worth the investment ... Our production manager wants to see more on-the-job management development ... Most middle managers are sceptical of management programmes because up to now they have been lecture-based and poorly delivered ... I get lots of consultants trying to sell me courses ... I had a meeting with the union representing many of our technical staff and they feel that their members should be given management training so they can understand the wider picture of what is going on.'

Listening to these comments, I was trying to build a picture of the network of forces on Phil Adams. We can see that already he is under pressure from various sources.

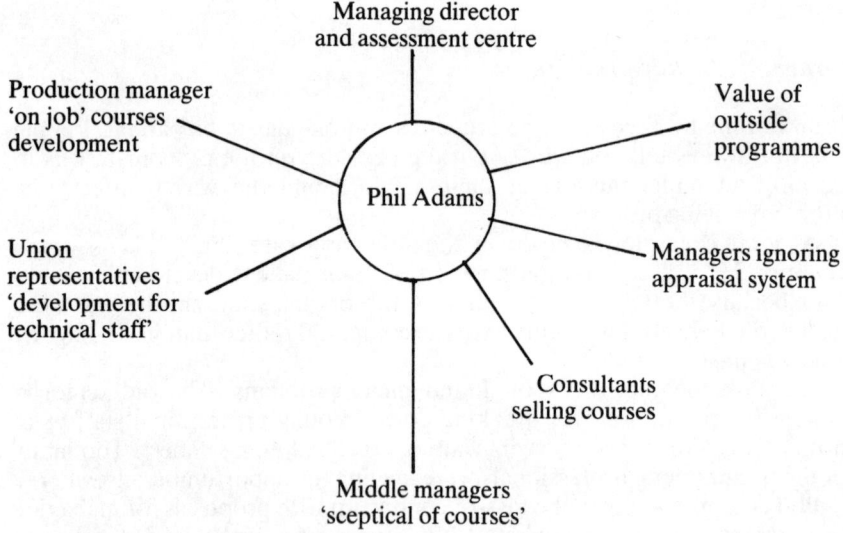

Establishing priority steps

All of this information is important but it does not tell you what Phil Adams should do. What questions would you ask Adams at this stage? Before reading on, make a list of the questions you would ask and the statements, if any, you would make. Would you ask questions on the areas he has already mentioned or ask him about areas he has not mentioned?

My own strategy in such situations is to search for information that the client is willing to give on the priority pressures in the network. This usually means getting the client to focus on the territory, time and permission and output issues. What does he need to do and by when, in order to satisfy someone or some people? This helps clarify where in the system the client should invest his limited time and energy. I try to get clients to point out who or what in their personal network is important within the foreseeable future.

What outputs are required?

Such questions as 'When do you have to report on the changes you propose?' or, 'Is there a timescale set for introducing any changes?' can be useful. In Phil Adams case they produced some interesting extra data showing how the system network around him was exerting particular time pressure.

Adams said, 'Well, there are a few outputs required. First, in order to get any money I have to submit a plan to the board within three months so we can get into the budgeting process. Second, there is a conference at corporate headquarters when I have to present our plan to other colleagues from the other companies and that takes place in four months. Third, the managing director asked me to form a management development committee and that has its first meeting next week. Finally, my own staff are looking for some direction on where to go from here.'

Suddenly, four time-based output pressures of strategic significance appear. Their place on the personal network of Phil Adams is crucial. Now the need for action is clear and the network, which I call the action network, is brought into sharper focus. This particularly showed up when I asked Adams which of these pressures was the top priority. He said the management development committee, because they need a strategy to put forward some new initiatives. We therefore started to discuss this in the context of the pressures he was under from others in the system. By talking through his pressure priorities and developing options, Phil Adams began to make a strategic approach to his job rather than just adapting *ad hoc* solutions.

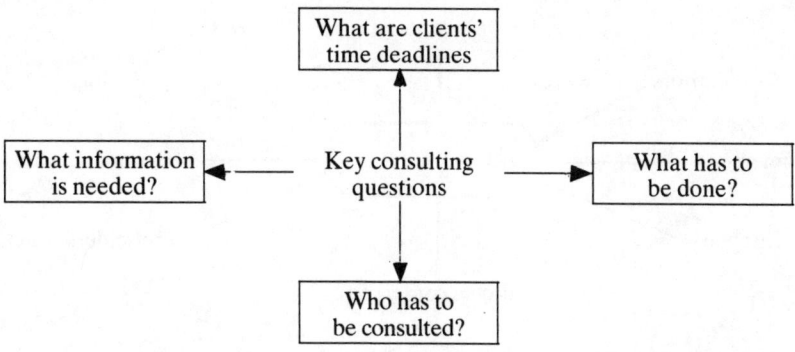

All clients are subject to role pressures like this. Unless you can do an action network analysis of their personal situation you may not find out where they or you should go next. This, to me, is all about understanding the place of the client in their open system.

How to visualize the issues

I am keen on asking clients to illustrate by diagrams and other visual aids how they see the problem. At the simplest level this usually means inviting them to draw an organizational chart of the characters concerned.

The formal organization chart is a good starting point. It provides a vehicle for talk. It legitimizes the visualization of the problem. It provides a basis for projecting their problem outwards.

Formal organizational charts seldom represent the real relationships. I encourage clients to amend the formal chart to show where the problem areas and the reporting and authority relationships exist.

As the client talks, I also take hold of the chalk and write key words or phrases next to his diagram. If the client makes a succinct statement of the problem, I will usually write this up.

While the best vehicle for visualization is usually a blackboard or an organization chart, it could be something else to which both parties can contribute. Many clients speak much more easily when they have a pen in their hands to illustrate the point on paper. Many feel more comfortable if they have some papers to which they can refer from time to time. These may seem small points, but they are the stage materials in the theatre of advice and must not be ignored.

It is therefore vital to develop a 'working model' with the client of the factors involved in the problem. Just as an architect develops a draft plan, so I try to work with the client to develop a draft analysis.

The context of change

All organizations are systems that live within a wider system of influences as shown below.

It is important to see the systems created by people in organizations as responses to these pressures, which are often seen as threats. It is difficult to understand any organizational system and change it effectively unless you and the client clearly diagnose the threats and opportunities from the wider system. Therefore a number of strategic planning consultants take this as their starting point.

When relating with an organization consider the wider system of which the part you are dealing is a part. For example:

- The individual is part of a chain of relationships with the boss, colleagues, his or her group. They may have competing loyalties such as the union v. the organization.
- The group is part of a wider network of other lateral and hierarchical groups whose work is influencing their action.
- The group is part of the corporate organization and needs to be seen in the context of wider policies.
- The organization, as illustrated above, is subject to pressures from many other community organizations and institutions.

If you wish to influence an organization look at where the fear factor is. What will happen if the people don't change? Will they be punished by prison, bankruptcy, job loss, shame? These are all great motivators for survival. So take systems seriously. They do have a real impact on change.

Below you will find some factors influencing change on organizational systems. Check which ones are having the biggest impact on you as a person and your organization.

Why do organizations change?

It helps if you can work with the forces of change rather than against, as it makes the process easier. Here are some common forces for changes.

- Outside pressure – government's loss of regulated markets.
- Opportunities – chance of winning important market, profit.
- Personal values and policy – beliefs of individuals which are strongly felt and imposed.
- Negotiation – union agreements.
- 'New broom' – new chief executive or managers making impact.
- Political conflict – the result of winning or losing a fight with suppliers, customers or staff.
- Market changes – customers voting with their money to buy or stay away.
- Research – innovators and new ideas.
- Keeping up with Jones's – not lagging behind the competition.
- What are the others you have experienced?

Guidelines

To be a successful adviser you need to discuss the context of the problem or opportunity facing the client. This means you need to look at the system rather than just the presenting symptoms. This requires skill in facilitating discussions on the role pressures faced by the client. It is that person who ultimately has to be accountable for the action.

Therefore your task should involve gaining permission to help explore territory relevant to the assignment. Don't seek information just for your own intellectual curiosity.

You should specifically raise open questions about:

- the client's own role pressures
- the forces in the system which he or she needs to work with or counter
- the outputs required
- the time deadlines set
- the expectations of others.

All of these factors provide the context within which the intervention has to be developed. If you do not understand these system factors it is likely your advice will be misdirected. If you help the client clarify his or her position in the system to meet the pressures, then that, in itself, can be a large contribution. We shall explore this in more depth in the next chapter.

Exercise

1   As a case example, what would be your strategy for advising Phil Adams on his next move, given he has said, 'The management development committee includes the production manager, the personnel manager, the marketing manager and a union representative. My main concern at the moment is how I can get this committee to work on the problem effectively. They are all very keen but it's a matter of knowing where best to start.'

2   Develop a visual of the system in which you conducted your last consulting assignment. How well did you deal with the issues?

12 Why role consultation is important

'Men at some time are masters of their fates;
The fault, dear Brutus, is not in our stars,
But in ourselves.'

Shakespeare, *Julius Caesar*

Knowing how to be an effective personal adviser means understanding how to undertake role consultation. This chapter outlines a specific example and draws out a number of points.

What is role pressure?

If I am consulted or asked to advise, I immediately look first to see what role pressure the client is under. It is important because:

- it will indicate what he expects of me
- it will tell me a lot about his own motivation, commitment and approach.

We are all under role pressure. It is a central factor in our lives. We have to develop skills in managing our lives where we play many roles, such as parent, boss, subordinate, friend, colleague, sportsman or representative. We often find ourselves in situations where it is difficult to perform one role without doing an injustice to the others. A working mother often has this problem when her child becomes ill. Should she go to work or stay at home to nurse the child? There is pressure from the employer to go to work but there is pressure from the child to stay at home. In the middle, the mother has to decide. She is under role pressure.

In organizational consulting the same thing occurs regularly. The manager is working in a field of counteracting forces. As the production manager he is pressed by the sales people for increased output, but the quality control people press him to keep to the standards and not risk lowering them by rushing the output.

Context or content

My own approach is to take the view that a client is in the centre of a competing set of pressures, based upon people's expectations of him. Some of these are clear and some are blurred. The first task is usually to work with the client to establish what their situation is. Do they want the adviser to work with them on the *context* or the *content* or both?

It is difficult to advise someone on what they should or should not do when the adviser does not know the role pressures they are under or their capacity to implement the advice. It is therefore preferable to start with the context diagnosis and look at the demands being made on the client, *vis-à-vis* their interests.

The role pressure network wheel is something you can use to help identify the strongest pressures. This is simply a diagram as shown which you can ask your client to draw or which you develop based on your knowledge of his or her situation.

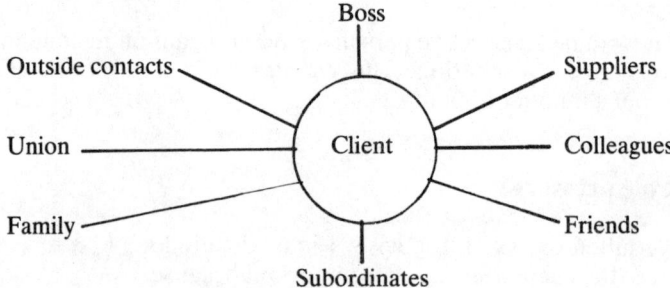

The innovation case example

In order to illustrate role consultation I have chosen a specific case. I was acting as an adviser to a group of people from different organizations who were on a management programme dealing with organizational innovation. Most of the participants were scientists concerned with research and development. This session was at the end of the programme, when we were dealing with the application of ideas to their organization. The aim of the session was to help members confront organizational role problems and develop helping and advisory skills amongst the members. One of the participants, George, had a number of problems. I have summarized the discussion as it highlights the importance of sensitive role consultation. As George outlined the problem, various group members tried to advise, and I have included their comments to illustrate how in the early part they missed the point by concentrating on technical rather than personal role issues.

Initial problem statement

'The people I work with are not very creative. They work hard on set jobs, but don't really generate new ideas. The problem is to get these people to extend their competence; become more co-operative and flexible in their work arrangements.' This is how George started the discussion.

The members of the group asked George a series of questions. What age were the people? How many of them were there? How long had they worked with the company? How were they rewarded? Were there any personality clashes? The questions continued.

Control discussion

I intervened to ask the group why they were asking George all these questions. The group felt it vital to know the details about the work and situation of the people referred to by George, so that they could help him. This is a common response. I confronted the group by asking them who they felt their questions were helping, themselves or George?

They felt that so far George had not been helped. Moreover, George agreed. We had been discussing the issue for nearly half an hour but not moving to solve the problem presented.

This particular incident throws into relief a number of cues that I look for when acting as an adviser.

Who is controlling the discussion? Invariably, the people asking the questions control the ground for discussion. They ask things that they want to know for their intellectual satisfaction, regardless of whether it has anything to do with the real problem.

Factor fixation

Witness in the case of George that people were asking about training, wages, ages, personalities and so on, almost to the length of people's hair and the colour of their eyes. These people are what I call *factor-fixated*. They are looking for the one factor that will provide the clue to the problem. They see the situation as analogous to solving a jigsaw puzzle. They are looking for the piece that is missing. They therefore seek to control the proceedings until they find what they regard as the vital factor.

However, the person with the knowledge of all factors is the client. It is my job to encourage him to control the proceedings. I therefore directed the participants' attention to the concepts of territory and interrogation. I asked them to stop interrogating the client. Instead I invited them to help the client explore his work territory; to think about his job, his position and his relationships, at his pace and in his own time.

The organizational map

One way of facilitating this is to invite the client to draw up the organization chart. On this occasion this is what George did. He drew it as follows:

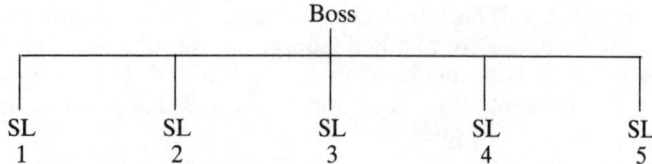

He suggested that the problem was that people were selected by the section leaders (SL) of each of these five groups, who were then reluctant to part with their men. The result was that people did not get experience of doing different work in other groups. They therefore had a narrow outlook and little creativity. He wanted to have cross fertilization between the groups. This clarified the problem somewhat, and again the group took up their consultation with George.

Closed-ended and solution centred questions

I had drawn attention to the fact that the group up to this point were asking closed-ended questions to which there were finite answers. Examples of this were the questions on how old the people involved were, and how long they had been with the company.

The other point I mentioned was that the group were asking solution-centred questions. For example, one member enquired: 'Why don't you establish a rota system and send round a note letting people know how you want the groups organized next year?' This is a common approach and early in discussion rarely helps matters. It closes the conversation down so that the client has to answer a specific point.

This solution-centred approach, unless requested, often leads the client to defend against the solution, rather than explore the problem. He becomes a victim of the helper who is over-keen to try out his solutions before an accurate diagnosis has been made. This may be a useful tactic when time is short. However, unless one has knowledge of the situation, which in most organizations is complex, the closed-ended solution-centred question is likely to lead to defensive behaviour from the client.

This time they let George control the proceedings by asking open questions. Why was it so difficult to change? George explained that the section leaders were all professional people of some influence who commanded the personal loyalty of those working with them. The conversation continued in this vein, with George talking about the section leaders and their men.

Who are we talking about?

At this point I again stopped the discussion to ask how people felt it was going. Opinions varied. I therefore enquired how far we were really understanding George's problem and position. It was agreed that so far George has been talking about *others*. This is a common issue in role consultation. The client will talk at one level removed. The effect is that we see others through him, but we do not hear of his relationship with them. The client talks as if he were detached. Clearly, this is not so. It is important for the consultant adviser to enable the client to talk of himself in the situation.

George was invited to show where he was on the organization chart. As on many such occasions, George had left himself off the chart. The redrawn chart looked as follows:

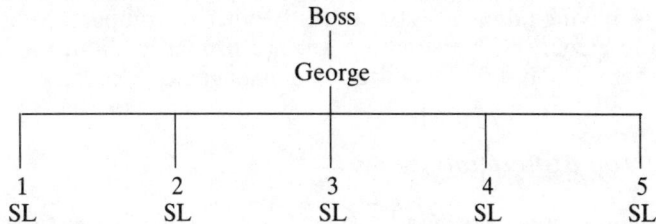

There was some surprise that George was so close to the problem. He had given the impression of being a detached observer. He was invited to describe his position in relation to the problem.

Personal involvement cues

It was here that George began to articulate his concerns much more keenly. He started drawing lines on the board to indicate points, he used his arms in gesticulation, the speed of his speech increased. All these were signs that George was now talking *about* the problem, rather than *to* the problem. It was at this point that he started using key words and phrases which I listen for when acting as a resource consultant. I have italicised cues as I heard them.

The key cues and clues

'You see, *the difficulty* is that *we cannot go on this way*. I have already had discussions with *my boss*. *He is new* to the job and *wants to see things organized differently. It is my job to produce an organization that is more flexible where people have experience in all five sections. I've ben given six months* to set up a planned development programme *for intersection exchange*, together with the formation of *project groups*, taking members from all sections. So far I've not got very far. You see, *I can't change the system* without *offending the section leaders* and *I depend on them* to get the work done. *If I did change to this new system it might not work.'*

For me, George was now getting near the real issue. He stopped talking about past events as a detached observer. He started to emphasize the pressures on himself at the present and the future objectives he must attain. We now saw George as the man in the middle of the stage, between his boss and the section leaders. George is on the verge of talking about himself and his job for the first time.

When a client starts to refer to himself in the problem, the consultant should pay extra special attention. It is not easy for most people to be self-critical in front of others. Therefore, when George started to say, "It's my job . . . I've been given six months to set up . . . so far I've not got very far . . . if I change the system it might not work,' then these are clear cues that the client is exploring the unknown and wants some assistance. George is making admissions about his feelings of competence in his job. Like many managers, his concerns are not primarily about the technical aspects of the job, but the organizational management aspects.

Personal role exploration

The problem is how to respond. 'Why must you have five sections?' asked one member of the group. I immediately intervened. This member was about to sidetrack the discussion. He was in a well-intentioned, but mis-leading, way going to open his own avenue of exploration. In a situation where the client is talking about himself in the first person singular then it is essential to stay with him. The intervention of the group member in my view was about to turn the conversation away from George and his role toward the inanimate sections and the reasons for their existence. I could see that within a couple of sentences we would have embarked on an entirely new route of exploration looking at how the sections came into existence, a detailed outline of what each section did and other issues relating to the sections.

Personal situation analysis

'How does your response relate to what George has just told us?' I asked the group member. 'Well, I thought that asking George if it was necessary to have five sections would help us solve the problem.'

'George has not asked us to solve his problem. He has, however, indicated an area he is prepared to talk about. It's our job to explore whether he wishes to talk more about that. The one way we can test this is to give him the opportunity to build on what he has said, and explore the alternatives available. To do this we can reflect in an open-ended way what George said to us at the end of his last contribution.'

No one could remember how George had finished his contribution. This in itself was instructive and the group clearly felt that they had not yet learnt to listen to what the client was saying. I emphasized to the group that it was essential to listen to where the client stops. He had not stopped talking because he has nothing else to say. He stops for a reason. The issues are: can he, and does he wish to, continue? At such a point the client stops to see if you are interested and if he can trust you. If you ask the right question in the appropriate manner he will continue.

I reflected back a paraphrase of his points: 'As I understand it, you feel that the present system works despite its disadvantages. Nevertheless, your boss is insisting on changes and you are not sure how to go about them in such a way that you get the co-operation of the section leaders.'

Client solution development

George replied, 'I have got some ideas of what we could do to develop more creative people in the sections, but it is not easy to introduce them. I would like to see a joint selection panel set up, rather than each section leader recruiting their people, and also introduce a project leader concept for temporary jobs that cut across section boundaries. Most of all, I believe that we need a planned personnel development programme so that people move between sections.'

It is now important to follow up and seek evidence to support the proposition put forward. In particular confront and challenge negative assumptions.

'How far do you feel able to discuss these issues with people at work?'

'Discussing them with the boss is no problem. He is all for the ideas. However, discussing them with the section leaders is a different matter. They would see it as breaking up their empires.'

Test negative assumptions positively

Here George makes a common move which many clients adopt. He puts forward negative assumptions. These are assumptions about other people's behaviour which he feels are opposed to his objectives. These negative assumptions must always be explored and tested. I asked the group how we could do this.

One member did this very well by saying to George: 'What makes you think the section leaders would feel you were breaking up their control?'

'It's hard to say,' said George. 'It's more an atmosphere. They are so bound up in the work of their section they don't consider the work going on in other sections. They seem blinkered in their thinking.'

'In what way have you tested this?'

'Well, each Monday morning I have half an hour's meeting with all section leaders to let them know of developments, work allocation and plans. During this time they let me know of the resources they require. Then during the week I make a habit of talking with each section leader for an hour to keep up to date on the work in each section. In these meetings we never seem to develop new ideas. Everyone is bound up with his little world.'

'You find it difficult to get them to communciate with each other?'

Sequential action discussion

Now each response was following on from what George was saying, we were having what I call sequential rather than parallel discussions.

'Yes,' said George. 'The meetings always get involved with the procedures and problems of the current jobs. We never seem to get time to talk generally about the future. In many ways I think that we need to abandon our formal agenda and have an open meeting like we are having now.'

'An informal meeting on how improvements in the working of the department can be made?'

'Yes, I need to get the section leaders together for, say, about two or three hours to look at how we improve our effectiveness. Maybe they have ideas which I haven't considered.'

Clarify the action steps

At this point George said he felt the discussion had been useful and he now had an idea of how to tackle his problems. He had not solved it, but he had thought out an approach different from that he had used. He was now going to put the general problem of how to improve the department's effectiveness to his section leaders. In doing this he was involving the very people who knew most about the problems and who could influence the implementation of ideas.

The breakthrough in George's thinking had been to set up a new form of meeting. As well as holding operational meetings to make short term decisions, he was now going to institute alongside these the long term planning meetings. Many clients find this distinction a helpful way of seeing a way to resolve a problem. However, an intellectual statement of the distinction is not in itself usually enough. The client needs to talk through his problem so that he sees the distinction for himself and is also able to formulate how he will initiate the new approach.

The phases of role consultation

In this role consultation we had gone through some typical phases. Initially you have to deal with the following points to discover the role pressures on George.

- Get the client to talk about his or her role.

- Avoid cul de sacs of intellectual interest to you but of no benefit to the client.
- Stick with his or her energy.
- Listen for the cue words and follow up.
- Ask questions rather than make statements.
- Deal with the past before asking about present and future.
- When you get facts ask for feelings and when you get feelings ask for facts.
- Enquire what the client will do next, when and with whom.

This specific case illustrates important points about the consultative process. You need to establish what the client is most concerned about. Initially they will probably describe the situation at 'arm's length', talking about 'them' and 'things' as if not personally involved. They will also probably talk mainly in the past rather than the present or future.

In such cases it is your job to encourage the client to discuss their role in the action and what they are doing now and will do in the future. If you can make that transfer you will have made an important contribution. This applies whether you are a manager acting as an adviser to a colleague or one of your staff, or an outside consultant.

Remember the conversation control model when dealing with such situations. There are two main options: You can either ask questions or make statements. These will be either problem oriented or solution oriented as shown below.

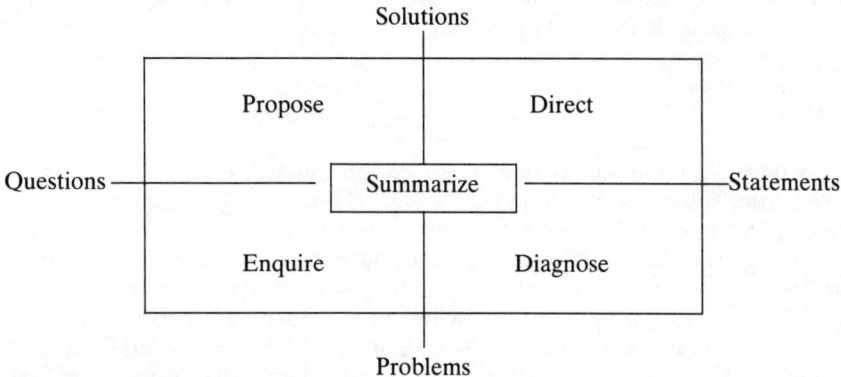

As a general rule the most appropriate steps will be to:

1 enquire
2 summarize
3 diagnose
4 propose
5 direct.

Often you will do the first three steps and the clients will do the last two. However, on occasions the client may ask you to put forward solutions to generate options. If so, pose them as questions. The important thing is to know what you are doing and enable the client to take action.

Work with the client you have with you

The person in the room at any particular moment should be your principal concern. Too often the person in your room is the one who is never talked about.

You can start either with presenting the symptoms or with the person who presents them. I try to start with the person who is with me. The answer to the problem may not lie with them, but the starting point for progress does. Remember to 'work with the client you have with you'.

Start with the person in front of you and work outwards. Do not encourage your contact to talk in a detached fashion about people 'out there' as if they were lost in a desert. Start with them and find out what he or she has done and wants to do about the problem.

This is a crucial point. You can waste vast amounts of time and money if it is ignored. Many advisers with considerable 'experience' still fail to recognize this. They proceed on a 'round the houses' basis, looking at virtually everything under the sun except the person closest to them.

All this is tied up with your advisory strategy. It implies that you are adopting a following style based on relevant questions. In the early stage of the relationship this is essential. So follow, but follow your contact at a personal level, not once removed. Keep asking yourself, 'what does my contact have to do next?' You won't go far wrong.

Guidelines

Too often, people inexperienced in consulting will come forward with premature solutions, stressing what others should do. Although it will take longer, you are more likely to get to the heart of the matter if you encourage the client to discuss what they have done, how they feel about it, and what they can do in the future. In this way you start with the problem and lead to the solution that the client perceives as feasible. That is important. They need to be clear in their mind what has to be done and confident they can do it. After all, it is still their problem to solve, not yours.

A useful checklist is:

- Ask the client what their role is in the proceedings.
- Enquire how events affect them personally.
- Find out first what has happened as a basis for discussing present and future action.
- Identify those who are putting the client under pressure.
- Listen for the key words.

- Help them think through who they must meet, when and how and what they will say to improve the situation.

Exercise

Consider a case when someone has come to you to discuss a specific problem. Review how you handled the assignment.

1 What was the issue?

2 In what ways did you get the client to discuss their own role?

3 What were the strengths and weaknesses of your approach?

4 What was the outcome?

Part IV
POLITICS AND PRESSURES

13　The politics of consulting

'There are two levers for moving men – interest and fear'

Napoleon Bonaparte

Power influences

Rarely is a consulting task simply a relationship between two people. When working on an advisory assignment with a large organization you invariably have to involve and gain the commitment of a number of people, in order for the project to succeed. These people may need to be incorporated into the organization structure of the assignment.

An assignment of any size involves a consideration of the politics of the assignment. At this point you have to consider where the power lies and how to mobilize it. This means having people on your side not just in attitude but also in action. It is therefore important to build a political structure to accommodate different interests and ambitions.

Many of the people who can influence the success or failure of an assignment don't have formal roles of authority within the organizational system. They may be opinion leaders. Others of course do have formal authority positions, and they or their representatives must be included.

The organizational arrangements need to be adjacent to but separate from the normal hierarchy of operations. There is a need for a temporary organization to manage the assignment where representatives can meet.

This organization structure can involve a steering committee, task forces, technical advisory groups or project teams. It is a group of people who meet specifically to guide and advise the consulting project.

All consulting assignments have to take place within an organization system. However, that system may not be sufficient for the management of a consulting assignment. Indeed, the very reason for the assignment may reflect the fact that the existing organizational structure does not cover the issues. It is important to establish the organizational structure of a consulting assignment at an early stage. This provides an opportunity for those who have interests in the project to be particularly represented, and to influence the processes taking place.

The steering committee structure

On an assignment that involves more than one or two people and will take place over some time, I like to establish a steering committee early on in the proceedings. The first time I introduced the steering committee approach was when working with a large telecommunications group. Although I and my colleagues had been asked to work on a large-scale project in the organization, concerning the development of engineers into a managerial role, there was still considerable scepticism and opposition to the project from many senior people. Though the board of directors had agreed on the need for the project and allocated the funds, there was a danger that our work could be undermined by senior technical people who felt that they did not have an influence upon proceedings. I thought it was important to have a meeting of these people to discuss how they saw the project, to identify their concerns and thus ensure their involvement.

The senior technical people felt that the project was being forced on them by the board of directors and we, as outsiders, were seen as people who knew nothing about their operation. During the meeting, numerous points emerged, but the overriding concern was that the senior technical people wanted to influence the direction of the project. I suggested that there be a steering committee which included people from their organization and our educational team who would join together to give their experience on the direction of the project.

Initially, the steering committee met about once a month during the design stage. Thereafter, it tended to meet on a quarterly basis. We ensured that there was an opportunity for the members of the steering committee to visit our place of work as well as our visits to them. Meetings were held alternately in their organization and in ours. This fostered a considerable amount of goodwill, as they began to understand our operations and we began to understand theirs. However, an important aspect of this was that we had begun to develop an organizational structure between our organizations. As I saw it, we had three levels. This threefold design

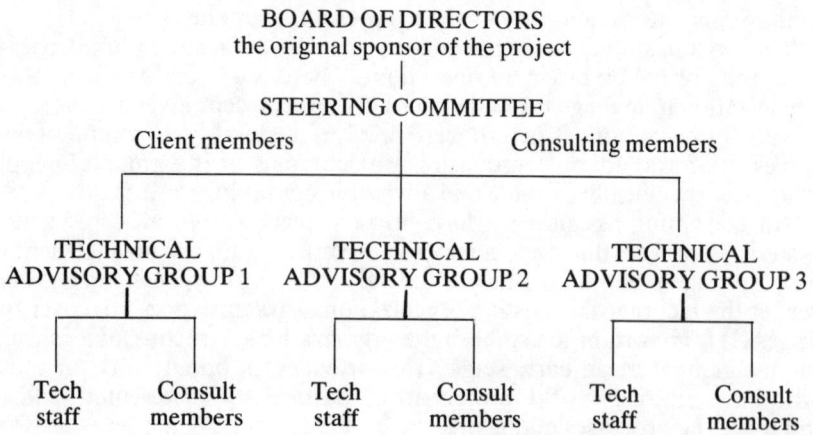

BOARD OF DIRECTORS
the original sponsor of the project

STEERING COMMITTEE
Client members   Consulting members

TECHNICAL   TECHNICAL   TECHNICAL
ADVISORY GROUP 1   ADVISORY GROUP 2   ADVISORY GROUP 3

Tech   Consult   Tech   Consult   Tech   Consult
staff   members   staff   members   staff   members

shows the complexity of organizational consulting in large projects. In addition to the three levels, there is also the end-user client. In this case, it was the senior departmental managers and their engineers who were nominated for a programme which was jointly run between their organization and ourselves.

The important point is that, in order to be successful at the educational level, it was vital to set up a political structure between the two organizations, so that adequate representation could take place.

The board of directors, having made a strategic decision, did not get involved apart from specific issues, when the managing director or one of his colleagues would attend a particular management programme to give an after dinner speech, or comment upon particular developments in the organization.

The steering committee consisted of those with an executive role and others with a political one, representing various parts of the company, as well as members of our own consulting team.

Technical advisory groups

The technical advisory groups consisted of individuals who mostly worked together on specific projects with our educational advisers. They did not meet as a committee. They tended to meet as and when required on specific tasks, and their activities were reported back to the steering committee. Their job was to gather the data necessary for the job to be done. This involved writing special papers, exercises and materials.

For example, one of the technical advisory groups worked on the topic of tariff pricing and how people could be taught to negotiate. This involved some of our staff working on a project basis with technical people from their organization. When the programme started it was interesting to note that this session was jointly taught by a member of the client organization and our own staff. This formed the model for much subsequent work where joint design and joint tuition were the order of the day, with technical and educational expertise linked together.

The political infrastructure

On the whole, the project ran well during a three-year period, at the end of which the company renegotiated the arrangements to continue for a further three years. I believe that the success of the project was largely due to the political infrastructure that was set up to enable people at various levels in both organizations to meet and talk about the various issues. If this had not happened, it would have been very difficult to have made progress, as senior technical people could well have withheld their support.

The politics of any consulting assignment are complex. I believe that we need to set up organization structures to cope with this complexity, rather than just deal with it on an *ad hoc* basis. When people can see that there is a formal structure that meets on a regular basis and to which they have access, they tend to use the structure rather than to fight rearguard battles.

This is not to say there is never any confrontation or disagreement. There is. However, it can occur in an open and constructive way so that both parties can discuss the problems and solve them. In this particular case, this was of considerable value to the board of directors, as well as the executives responsible for making the system work, who did not have, within the existing company structure, a political base from which to proceed. The steering committee system that we established became their political base for involving people and gaining commitment to new ideas and projects.

There are occasions, however, when the steering committee are the main actors in the drama. This often happens when you are consulting with a team that has to make the decision rather than making recommendations to others. In such cases it is important to look at another facet of managing consulting assignments – that of stakeholder analysis.

The stakeholders system

Stakeholders are people and organizations associated directly or indirectly with an assignment who stand to lose or gain by the actions taken. They can be internal stakeholders as shown in the above case or external stakeholders. It is important to know who the stakeholders are as this can be helpful in structuring discussions and formulating action.

A good example of identifying stakeholders emerged in my work with a large energy company. The organization had made a big capital investment in a gas pipeline. However, one of the major buyers of the gas decided to postpone its purchase for at least three months and possibly permanently. This was a great setback for the company, as it had made great commitments in terms of capital and people. I was asked to work with the senior team to look at the implications. What would be the consequences if this important purchaser, which had planned to take 80 percent of the company's supply, postponed its purchase? Without this particular client, the project looked as if it could be wasted, as there was no other potential buyer for the energy.

The senior management group therefore met to discuss what needed to be done. Initially there was a depressed atmosphere. It was important to have a positive approach to the problem. The general manager therefore began his introduction by saying: 'We must look to ways in which we can respond to this problem so that we regain the initiative.' He did not blame anyone for the contract going wrong, nor did he dwell upon the past, and the reasons associated with the change. He concentrated exclusively on the present difficulty and future action that needed to be taken.

He then indicated that he wanted me to help facilitate this discussion. We talked about the way in which we could best approach the matter. It was agreed that there were a number of people and organizations with interests in the company, so I suggested we do a stakeholder analysis to identify the key actors involved and to determine how best to work with them to resolve the problem.

Below is the model we constructed.

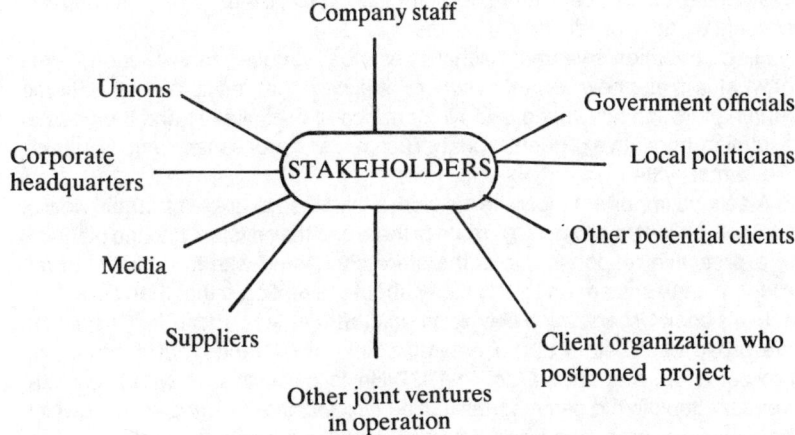

These were the principal stakeholders as seen by the senior managers on a first analysis. It was agreed that it was important to contact as many of these stakeholders as possible to inform them of the present situation, in order to influence their thinking and decision making. I asked which of the stakeholders they regarded as the main priority. It was generally agreed that the government politicians and administrators were the key stakeholders.

We drew up a set of points and questions that needed to be raised with people in both the political and administrative side of government. As a result of doing this, we were then able to ascertain which people should be contacted. Each of the senior managers wrote down the person or persons they would talk to and it was agreed that they should meet again as a team, within one week, to report back.

The team then looked at other aspects of the problem and selected other areas which they felt were important. A number of senior managers felt it was vital that the media be informed in such a way that the implications for unemployment were dealt with. This was agreed upon and accountability assigned.

Equally, it was felt that people who were supplying the company with materials, and whose business and employment could be affected, should be informed as early as possible, in order to reduce any problems.

Within a relatively short period, senior management had developed a stakeholder plan for dealing with the crisis. This had not solved the main problem. However, it had produced a concerted way of tackling the issues raised by the crisis. One manager said when we broke, 'That was a really useful meeting. I wish all our meetings were as well organized and productive as that one.'

Organization development strategies

Beckhard (1969) has been operating as an external consultant in private practice for over two decades. He has been particularly influential in developing the concept and practice of organization development and the associated advisory skills.

His contribution is valuable in that it describes various interventions in terms of what is done, how, when, by whom and with what result. A central theme running through his writing is the importance of consultation and the need to establish innovative organizational structures and processes (usually outside the formal system).

A second important theme in his work is the need to take a strategic view of where the client is going, the threats to them and their system and the planning of a proactive response. He is therefore concerned with the 'health' of the client and the system and particularly about prevention rather than cure.

In his book *Organization Developments: Strategies and Models*, he set out the broad parameters of the emerging field of OD and what a consultant adviser could and should do. In 1977 He followed this up with a complementary book in the same series, called *Organizational Transitions*, in which he outlined approaches for dealing with complex change.

Three points he stresses are:

1   the need for a good diagnosis of the conditions causing a need for change
2   a detailed picture of a desired end state
3   a clear and accurate picture of the dynamics of the present.

Beckhard combines the wide strategic approach to consulting with showing the importance of the middle ground of setting up consultative structures, but he leaves the detailed micro interpersonal interactions for others to outline. His focus is primarily that of the manager, and particularly top management, to help them 'understand the process of change and to have a better idea of what is required to facilitate and improve that process'.

Whose side are you on?

An important aspect of the politics of consulting is who are you for and who are you against. Consultancy advisory work usually involves the taking of sides. Therefore at the commencement of a project, it is important to determine whether you should take sides and, if so, whose side you are on. In essence, a consultancy project involves you – as consultant adviser – assisting a group or individual in terms of work performance.

The mediation case

The need to recognize whose side you are on became a reality to me when I was asked to mediate in an industrial dispute. I received a telephone call from a senior manager in the organization that a strike was threatened unless a solution could be found to an industrial relations problem. My contact, whom I had not met before, said that a factory operative had been sacked because he had been absent from his workplace without permission. The employee admitted that he had gone outside the factory to get some food and left his machine unattended. The management alleged that he had broken rules and created a safety hazard. The union alleged that management was exaggerating the situation in order to get rid of an employee they did not want.

The dispute had gone through the normal channels and had now reached a serious situation. Despite much internal discussion, no resolution had occurred, and the full-time union officials had failed to reach an agreement with the management. However, both the union and the management had agreed to a mediator. The idea was that the mediator should listen to both sides and then come up with a recommendation. However, neither party was prepared to agree in advance to whatever the mediator might propose.

I had read the documents pertaining to the problem and I had talked on the phone with the senior industrial relations person, who seemed under pressure, so I promised to meet both sides as quickly as possible. He was the only person I talked to prior to going to the factory.

Initial error

Due to a lack of thought, I made a serious error as I entered the factory. The only person's name I had was the senior manager with whom I had talked on the phone. At the factory gate I asked the security man for this person. He directed me to the offices, on the third floor. I went up and knocked at the door of the manager concerned. He greeted me and immediately said, 'I'm pleased you got here on time. Before we go into the meeting with the unions it would be useful if you could meet the managing director and our senior production manager, who will be at the meeting today.'

Of course, at this point I should have realized the danger. However, I was not thinking whose side I was on. In fact, in this particular situation it was inappropriate for the mediator to be on anyone's side, even if only by association.

My contact took me to the managing director's office where I met him, the senior production manager, and the personnel manager. They talked briefly about the case and expressed their views. By the time this was done it was time for the meeting. My contact, together with the other managers, said that we should go immediately to the office where the union people had already assembled.

Identification by association

Still I was not thinking clearly. My direct involvement with senior management prior to the mediation could be interpreted as colluding. The reality of this only hit me as I walked through the door into the office where all of the union people were assembled. As I walked in, sandwiched between the senior management team, I immediately recognized that I was identified as one of them. No longer was I seen to be independent. I tried quickly to overcome the error by moving myself into a position at the table between the union people and the management team.

However, the union people were suspicious and started asking questions about how far I had been briefed or, as they might see it, 'nobbled', by the management.

An argument broke out early, between union and management people, on how the proceedings should be conducted. I tried my best to get them to problem-solve this procedural issue, but already we seemed at an impasse. I remember saying that, although I had had a pre-meeting with the management team, we had not discussed the issue in substance (which was correct) and said that my aim was to mediate, rather than stand in judgement as to which side was correct. After this and other matters had been discussed, it was agreed that I should see the union people separately from the management people, and only have a joint meeting after both sides had the opportunity to talk with me.

Independent conciliation

The next six hours were spent locked up in a cell-like room. I was visited at regular intervals by people from the union and later by people from management. Meals and drinks were passed to me as if I was in quarantine. Each side tried to convince me that they were in the right. The unions insisted that the man had to be re-employed. Management insisted that he was sacked and could not be reinstated.

At the end of the day I called both groups together to summarize the issues as I had heard them. I said that my understanding was that, while the man was sacked, he could reapply for his job and be reappointed if he agreed to certain conditions. Management insisted he could not be reinstated on the previous terms. Eventually the union people accepted this, as they had established the principle that the man could work at the organization again.

I remember this case well because it taught me that, if I am mediating, then right from the beginning I must be independent. I had, by association, compromised my independence and only managed to retrieve it through being open about the process of my introduction into the organization. Thereafter, I had to prove that I was independent by the way in which I conducted the discussions with both sides. Eventually, the union accepted that I was not in the pocket of management, although I was being paid by them to help resolve the dispute. The lesson to me was that if you intend to mediate you must be independent right from the beginning.

Recognize the sides

When you are *not* mediating but problem solving, you are still taking sides. By working for one group, rather than another, you give your time and help to resolve a problem in that group's favour. That is why I believe it is important that we look at whom we work for and why we do particular jobs. There have been occasions on which I have refused assignments and these reflect the principles that one brings to the assignment. People who employ me and reward me for help are asking me to be on their side. While this may be so, I nevertheless seek to adopt the problem-solving rather than confrontation approach in overcoming any difficulties.

While I cannot stand in the middle, I can help those people who have differences to resolve them in a problem-solving way, rather than by simple disputation over who has the greatest power at any particular point. Knowing whose side you are on at any one time is important. It provides a basis upon which you can facilitate and help the problem-solving process.

Guidelines

All consulting assignments are political events. You are choosing to intervene. In the process you will be asked to take sides in some shape or form. The fact that you are using your time for the benefit of one person or group means you are lending your weight to their cause. Even when you are acting as a mediator you will find the pressure on you to take sides. While it is important to be impartial it is difficult.

Identifying the total organizational system within which the assignment is being conducted is helpful in structuring discussions and subsequent action, when a problem seems difficult and involved. A consultant adviser can help clients think about what are the key questions, and can thus provide the basis for a positive problem solving situation.

The steering committee is an excellent mechanism for involving people with different interests and roles. It provides a separate pitch to discuss issues where everyone can meet and seek to resolve the political issues.

Likewise the stakeholder model, in this particular case, is a useful one. In essence, it means identifying all the individuals and groups who will be affected by a certain decision so that everyone involved in the political implications can be consulted.

By enabling the group to focus on each of the stakeholders and what the implications are for them, it is possible to start thinking of the action required. However, it is equally important that the adviser stresses, not only the questions that need to be asked, but who will actually take action, by going out and talking with others. Equally, it is important to pick a date on which everyone can report back, so that there is a clear timescale within which people have to achieve their work tasks.

The mediation structure is often the most difficult political role involvement for a consultant adviser. It is hard not to be seen taking sides. In such situations the process consulting skills are demanded so that the participants come to a conclusion amongst themselves if possible.

Exercise

1   What structures have you used to deal with the political issues in an assignment?

2   Construct a stakeholder model for one of your projects, listing individual contacts.

3   What rules or principles do you establish when involved in a mediating role?

14 How to involve the make or break people

'Where's the man who counsel can bestow; still pleased to teach and yet not proud to know.'

Alexander Pope

Identify the sources of influence

It is easy to lose an assignment but difficult to gain one. I have found in most of my work there are people who can make or break an assignment. It is important to find out quickly who they are and involve them at the early stages.

Question assumptions

I was asked by a leading bank to design a training programme for their branch managers. It was a sizeable assignment as the bank had 70,000 employees in over 3,000 branches. The bank wanted its managers to be better at marketing and also at handling staff relations, particularly those involved in dealing with unions.

From a technical point of view the design of the course content was not very difficult. From a political viewpoint it was a very complex situation. My point of contact was the central training department. They were keen to get the programme started at the least cost.

We were already working in some detail when I felt that we were ignoring people who could influence the outcome. I asked, 'Who do the branch managers, who will be coming on this programme, report to?'

'They report to area managers', replied my contact.

'Have they been consulted about the proposed training?' I asked.

'They know about it, as it has been raised at senior manager meetings.'

I sensed that we were proceeding on an assumption that, because people knew about it, they would therefore support it. This is a dangerous assumption. I asked, 'Do you feel we should involve the area managers at all in our assessment of needs?'

The training person from head office thought it would be useful and we should send them a letter. I felt we should go further than that and invite them to a planning workshop.

'They won't come,' said my contact. 'They are too busy.' I felt this assumption should be tested, and asked him if it would be acceptable if I invited a representative group. He agreed.

The result was a turning point in the assignment. Not only did the area managers attend a two-day planning workshop, but they also brought numerous good ideas. As a result we agreed to have a follow-up meeting to feedback the design of the event and to enable them to test out key points of the programme. At this meeting most area managers brought along one of their branch managers also. They participated and gave valuable feedback which we incorporated in the design.

Line support

The programme was then run. We trained the bank's own staff to run it and it became a considerable success. Many months later I was invited to the bank's head office by the general manager in charge, as a mark of appreciation. At the lunch he congratulated us on the work that had been done. However, in the private discussions with me he said, 'The most important thing in making this programme a success is the support given by the area managers.'

If we had not involved them at an early stage I do not believe we would have had their political support and commitment. Moreover, I don't believe the programme would have been as well designed, because their experience contributed so much. They were in this case the make or break people.

In every assignment you will find people who need to be consulted if you are to succeed. So many have to be involved for diplomatic reasons even though they can contribute little to the technical side. Others need to be involved because they not only carry a lot of authority in the system but also have a wealth of experience to contribute.

Union support

I found this when working in the aviation industry with pilots. Although management commissioned us to design a team development workshop for the crews of Boeing 727, DC9, and the Airbus 300, there were powerful individuals in the system who could make or break the assignment. Most of these people had union roles in either the pilots' federation or the flight engineers' association. I therefore took time to involve them and listen carefully to what they thought. They had good ideas but much initial suspicion. Once we had started to understand their concerns and build the programme in such a way as to integrate those points, the representatives became enthusiastic supporters. At their respective union meetings they spoke up for the programme and ensured it got the political support required.

Advisory support

In many assignments you cannot progress unless you gain the support of people who act as gatekeepers. They don't actually control the budget, nor are they in an authority position. They do, however, control the advice the decision makers get.

This is most notable in dealing with government agencies. It is usually difficult to get to see the Minister or other senior elected officials. You first have to go through the appointed bureaucrats whose job it is to vet your proposals. It can take a long time to gain their advisory support before they will open the gates to the decision makers. It takes patience and persistence as well as skill.

In industry the same phenomenon occurs. I work a great deal in the training area. I therefore take a lot of time to ensure that the management development manager is aware of what I am proposing even though he or she may not make the final decision. They can influence it one way or the other with their advice.

From time to time such advice may not be what you as a consultant want. I made the mistake on one important assignment of putting all the information I had to just one person in the organization. I assumed he would send it to the decision makers. It was a very wrong assumption.

Therefore, don't let advisers get in your way. Wherever possible, make sure the information you give them does not gather dust on their desk or get mis-translated. Make every effort to pass your data directly to the people who can decide rather than just advise.

Consultants and their models

Every consultant has a model or theory of how to influence people underlying their practice. Some outline their principles and we have summarized a few of the leading managerial consulting theorists in these summary sections throughout the book. Other consultant advisers worthy of mention in brief as their principles have had an impact are:

Carl Rogers: He emphasized the importance of non directive counselling and advice. His basic message was that the consultant should not be offering solutions, but asking questions to help the client think out the answer for themselves. He assumed that once people had greater understanding of their feelings then it was likely they could become more effective. Rogers (1951, 1958) felt that people could gain control of their own lives if they are given the opportunity to reflect on where they have been, where they are and where they want to be. This reflection could be aided by non directive counselling and provide the motivation to purposeful action.

B. F. Skinner: He had a very different approach developed from the original work of Pavlov. He considers everyone's behaviour is shaped and conditioned by various stimuli. He coined the term operant conditioning. This term signifies that certain conditions will make it highly likely people will behave in certain ways. Skinner (1971) believes that behaviour is a function of the likely consequences arising. Therefore he advocates teachers and other consultants pay attention to the physical structure and reward systems that can influence behaviour. He has been accused of advocating the setting up of 'manipulative situations'. Skinner argues that such conditions are there in everyday life and it is just an ethical question of how we use them.

V. Frankel: He spent many years in a Nazi concentration camp. He argues he survived because he developed a strong set of purposes. His beliefs in these purposes, he argues, kept him going when others who felt they had little to live and fight for gave in to the oppressors. After his release he established a consulting practice called 'logotherapy' (1973). He worked with his clients to help them develop and establish important purposes in their life and work towards them.

These three approaches of non directive counselling, operant conditioning and logotherapy are all very different in approach and again show the wide range of consulting theory and practice.

How plans go wrong

At the beginning of a consultancy advisory assignment there is usually considerable energy being exerted to get a project under way. The client will have identified an area that needs to be improved and will want to work with you, the consultant adviser, to get something going. In my experience, however, the client does not always involve other critical people in this decision and this can have a negative effect upon the ultimate outcome. Indeed in many cases it can actually ruin the project. Great expectations can be unfulfilled unless the consultant adviser monitors the situation from the outset, and doesn't overlook vital aspects of the project.

The drinks galore case

A good example of this comes from a large company manufacturing a range of drinks. I had originally met the sales manager on a course and he later rang me to suggest that we meet and discuss specific issues relating to his sales team. He was concerned that with the rapid growth in the business there was a danger that things would get out of control. In particular, it emerged, he was specifically concerned about his own managerial skills. He had been promoted from a salesman to take over the sales team at a time of rapid expansion. He found that he was working 15 and 16 hours a day but still having serious problems.

The sales team was organized in two groups. One was based at head office and the other in a city 500 miles away. The sales manager had little opportunity to meet some members of the sales team, who were geographically widespread. He therefore decided to hold a conference in which he got the whole team together to discuss the problems they were facing and ways in which they could improve the work process. He did not wish the conference to be a series of talks from experts and senior managers. He was concerned that the sales people themselves should say what they thought and have an opportunity to influence the direction in which he was managing. He seemed to me to be an open-minded manager who had the energy and personality to accept whatever came up and work with it.

Project plan stages

I suggested to him that the approach should be to gather the views of the sales people prior to any conference and design the agenda around the issues they raised. We again used the steps and stages model which enabled the sales manager to see specifically how this would move forward. I proposed the following approach:

1 I would meet with head office sales staff as a group and talk over the points that they thought were of importance.
2 I would meet with the sales group in the northern city and discuss with them the key issues.
3 I would develop a report and plan for the conference which could be debated by both groups.
4 The plan was to organize the conference over a period of three days so that the issues raised could be discussed in detail, as well as having some senior managers attend to talk about policy issues.
5 I agreed to write a report on the proceedings as a basis for executive action by the sales manager and his team.

These five stages were agreed to by the sales manager and he arranged for me to meet with the sales team at head office. The meeting took place on Monday morning and the salesmen had been briefed that I would be attending. However, they had no idea of the specific points to be discussed. The sales manager introduced me and then left the room, saying it would be best if I talked with people without him being present. Again I felt this reflected the open way in which he was managing the operation. During the morning the salesmen gradually opened up and started to talk about their real concerns and issues, about the way things were managed in the organization.

Some important points began to emerge. These included:

Merchandising and expenses: The sales people had been asked to get involved in merchandising and this, it was felt, slowed down the number of their sales calls and increased expenses. It was felt that the company was mean when it came to expenses and one member said, 'We have not had a review for a number of years.'

Field visits: It was felt that the sales manager, because he was so busy, did not have the time to visit people in the field and did not understand the current problems they were facing.

Sales meetings: It was felt that the sales meetings did not really get down to the real issues because of the lack of time and they were used purely for passing on information.

Information and trust: Beyond these matters the sales people were concerned that they 'did not have enough discretion in dealing with discounts'. They had to refer to head office every time they wanted to give a concession to a client. 'We are often treated as if we are employed by the opposition,' said one salesman. Another person said, 'Too often we are getting information back from the licensees who tell us things that we should know.'

The list of salesmen's concerns centred on the central question of how far management trusted them to do a professional job. A great deal of energy and emotion was raised at the meeting. All of these points were re-echoed when I met with the team from the northern group. As a result of these meetings I wrote a report to the sales manager outlining the concerns and quoting comments without divulging names.

How breakdown occurred

When we met to discuss this report he agreed that it supported his view that it was essential to get the sales conference together as quickly as possible to discuss these matters. We arranged a date and fixed a venue. Then things began to go wrong.

In order to proceed he had to have the agreement of the general manager. A budget had been previously allocated. However, the general manager had seen the sales conference as a training exercise. When the plan was put to him for a sales conference that did not have any specific training sessions but dealt entirely with matters raised by the salesmen, he reacted negatively.

He went even further than this. He said that he had been talking with other organizations about sales training. He had seen what had happened in other places and felt strongly that the company should buy a sales training system for its salesmen. He introduced the sales manager to the training people at corporate headquarters, who had already introduced a package system in the wider company.

Dealing with the negative response

A few days later I received a telephone call to say that the sales conference was off. The sales manager had been forced to go along with the general manager's view about a sales training course.

This, as you can imagine, left the sales manager in a difficult situation. Not only did he feel that he had to apologize to me but, more important, he had to tell all of his sales team that the sales conference was no longer on.

Great expectations had been aroused in the salesmen, who felt for the first time they were going to discuss the real issues involved in their work. Now they were going to be sent on a packaged training programme. The sales manager felt that considerable energy and excitement had been raised, and that the general manager had cut across his area and ruined his plans.

The whole exercise up to this point had been conducted professionally on both sides. The sales manager and his staff had been involved at all stages. However, the project came to a grinding halt. What went wrong? Great expectations were unfulfilled and the sales manager felt embarrassed and caught between two different approaches.

How a client shows resistance

- Yes, but's
- Talking of others, not self
- Changing the subject
- Missing meetings
- Passing responsibility to you for his problem
- Intellectualizing
- Attaching
- Withdrawing
- Avoiding the question
- Defensive body movements

Action required

If you had been involved in such an assignment, what would you have done? Would you have consulted the general manager at an earlier stage? Would you have advised the sales manager to check out his plan with the general manager first? Would you advise the sales manager to continue with his plans but delay them for a while? Would you keep your advice and your feelings to yourself?

Guidelines

Whenever you work with large organizations, try to discover who are the people who can 'make or break' your project. Involve them in discussing what is required, and use their experience. Feed back to them what they have said and use that information as the basis for design. Bring them together and let them see what you have done.

Initially, you might find resistance in getting these people together. People will tell you they are too busy. People will find all sorts of excuses. However, you can be certain that if the project personally affects the people who can 'make or break' the programme, because it affects their role, then they will find time to attend.

Questions that advisers can use

- Who should be involved in discussion?
- How should we meet – separately or together?
- What data should we collect?
- Who should receive the data?
- What is the plan for using the data?
- What do you feel are the consequences of not doing anything?
- What are the pressures on you?
- Who will lose and who will benefit from the changes?
- Whose problem is it?

Exercise

1   Think about a time when you have had a breakdown on a consulting assignment. What happened?

2   What do you do to ensure breakdowns don't occur? What systems do you have?

15 The actors and their scripts

'All the world's a stage,
And all the men and women merely players:
They have their exits and their entrances;
And one man in his time plays many parts.'

William Shakespeare, *As You Like It*

The main actors

It is vital for the consultant adviser to be able to identify the client's system and where he or she fits into this system. In all organizations one can see the drama of everyday life. In effect, there is a play occurring on stage and there are various actors playing out particular roles. They either write their own scripts or have them written for them. During the course of a day, a week, a month, or a year, the various acts and scenes link to the plots and themes of organizational life. But just as an actor can be unsuitable for a certain part, so can members of an organization play roles that are unnecessary or unfulfilling, or write scripts and plots that are unfit for the drama of organizational life.

At the beginning of any assignment I ask the client to identify the main actors. This can be done in various ways, such as asking the client to draw a picture of the people involved in the organization. This is usually far more enlightening than looking at formal organizational charts. The actual pictures that people draw give clues. Also, in producing the drawing, the clients are raising their energy levels and are able to contribute in a positive way to the diagnosis. In such a presentation, they will invariably give some information, not only on the task problems involved, but the personalities.

Scripts, plots and themes

From this, you can begin to read the scripts, plots, and themes, the reasons underlying your original invitation and the organization, and the drama which is unfolding. It is the interaction between the various actors involved that is important in diagnosis. Usually the problems relate to the fact that the actors are not communicating properly with each other.

171

Either their scripts prevent them from communicating, or they are developing plots which limit accurate and open communication.

The important point is to listen to what people say about the actors and scripts, without judging them. I in no way seek to evaluate what people say about the actors and the scripts and the organizational play in which they are involved. My task, firstly, is to have them verbalize what they see as the issue and, in doing so, help them to understand their roles more clearly by putting words to their feelings.

I am always amazed, in listening to clients talk about the organization in which they are involved, that they rarely, if ever, describe accurately what their own roles are. Even when I have asked them to draw an organizational picture, I usually find they leave themselves out.

The roles in the play

I therefore ask the rather obvious but straightforward question, 'Where do you fit into this organizational picture?' or I ask, 'How does this issue affect you personally?' Usually I get an interesting reply, which goes something along the following lines:

'Well, that's an interesting point. You see, I've shown the relationship between these two departments. My job is in between these two departments but I don't have any authority over either of them. For me to do a good job means that they have to cooperate with me. However, they are so busy making life difficult for each other and pursuing their separate objectives that I get lost in the middle. In fact, it's worse than that. I'm often the only source of communication between the departments and can therefore be accused of creating problems rather than resolving them.'

This is a typical illustration of the sort of points that clients have raised with me. If I hadn't asked a straightforward question of where my client fitted in, I might have received a totally distorted picture of the conflict in the organization. Initially, I had been invited to consult on how to bring these two departments together. However, by listening to my client, I began to realize that was exactly the role that he had in the system. However, the scripts being played by the other two departments meant that it was difficult for him to play this role. He had therefore asked me to come and assist in the process.

Getting people to meet

What should one do in such situations? It is easy to say 'Bring the two departments together and get them to talk about the issues.' This in itself seems the obvious solution, therefore it may not be the obvious way to start tackling the problem. Instead, I would normally try to encourage clients to talk more about the roles they play in the organizational drama, the scripts they have had in the past, and what they wish to have in the future. The conversation may run as follows:

Myself: How much do people from these different departments meet?
Client: They meet quite regularly. That is where most of their differences are aired. They have a weekly business meeting in which
they discuss how operations are proceeding.
Myself: Are you involved in that?
Client: Not at all. I am never invited to the meetings. I am seen as a
separate part of the organization, concerned with training and
development, rather than part of line operations. The two
departments in question, credit control and marketing, are
operational departments rather than service departments, such
as myself.
Myself: How useful would it be to attend their meetings?
Client: I think it would be very useful. All I get at the moment are the
minutes, and the individual members complaining to me about
what a waste of time their meetings are.

Facilitating meetings

It is clear my client is in a difficult situation. The two groups meet regularly, but still do not seem to resolve their problems. Therefore, on the
surface, calling another meeting does not seem to be the answer. He has
said that it would be useful if he attended their meetings. This is a cue
which can be followed up. However, it is important to develop a script for
the client with which he feels confident and capable of implementing. At
this stage, the client feels rather frustrated because the script that he has
been using is not working and the role he feels he should perform is not
being implemented.

In this particular situation, the client felt it would be appropriate if he
facilitated a non-operational meeting with the key parties in the departments, but was not sure how to do this. I discussed the various options
available including interviewing the individual members of the departments prior to a meeting, and putting down some of the questions that they
all felt should be resolved. This he eventually felt confident enough to do,
and facilitated what was felt to be a most useful and productive meeting
with the departments.

Looking back on such incidents in an organization, where we have actors
and scripts, the action taken seems to be rather obvious. However, at the
time, it is definitely not obvious.

In all consultancy advisory work there are people who are playing
particular roles as actors in an organizational drama. They have scripts,
and may be working with others to pursue a particular plot which, in
organizational terms, we elevate to the concept of objectives. The meetings that take place, or do not take place, are just part of the various acts
and stages in the drama. The good consultant adviser seeks to discover the
roles that people are playing and enables individuals to work together in a
more authentic way, rather than hiding behind their roles and scripts. In
one sense, consultant advisers are helping to rewrite organizational

dramas. In this way, they act not so much as the playwright, but as the director of the play.

Learn from mistakes

We can all learn from mistakes providing they are not too big and we think through what we can do better next time. In order to improve listen to what others have done and see how you can improve.

In that context it is useful to reflect on Reddin's (1977) main reasons why he 'failed' on some assignments but from which he learnt how to improve. These I have summarized with my own brief interpretation.

Bottom up change: trying to make radical changes by lighting revolutionary fires down below. The change if it occurs is unlikely to be easy or planned.

Creating change overload: too much, too soon, too often. The result is that people back off.

Raising expectations beyond what is possible: many promises and not much fulfilment create widespread dissatisfaction.

Inappropriate attachment: linking into the wrong part of the system or becoming too attached to a person who can't move things on.

Becoming trapped in one part: extension of the above but being identified too closely with one part of the organization.

Changing only a subsystem: not getting to the main centre of the action but having a great success in a small unit.

Inappropriate intervention: maybe trying to change the people before the structure and strategy or vice versa.

Assuming change is needed: maybe it is not and the new is not better than the old.

Failing to seek help: the adviser is supposed to provide help, not seek it, but this may be the source of his or her failure.

The theatre of organizational consulting

I have found the analogy of the organization as a theatre, in which various dramas take place, very helpful. In particular, I have discussed this analogy with clients, and they have adopted it very quickly. However, it is most important, in doing this, not to typecast people, but to use the analogy as a way of illustrating the realities. An integral part of this is to encourage the clients to talk about their roles, their feelings about their scripts and the way in which they wish to change their performance. In doing this, one can then move more successfully from past behaviour to future improvements.

In all consulting assignments you have to establish an understanding of the actors, their roles and their scripts. This means recognizing the system in which they work and their own personal network they seek to influence and that seeks to pressure them. This will involve an understanding of the territorial arrangements to establish who controls what and how. You will need to be active in gaining permission to cross territorial boundaries where necessary in order to do your job, particularly when it means facilitating problem solving between two or more units. Iain Mangham (1979) has written extensively about this approach to organizational analysis. In a different way Charles Handy (1979) has made similar valuable insights through his use of Greek and Roman history in his book *Gods of Management*.

Case study of organization drama

So many of the assignments in which consultant advisers are involved centre around personalities and politics. In almost every case the adviser knows little or nothing of the personalities, and less of the politics. Nevertheless, people ask advice and seek guidance on how to handle such matters. Why should they do this when the adviser is less knowledgeable than they of the details of the situation? To what extent can a consultant help others with the personalities and politics involved in an organization?

An example of personalities and politics in consulting is the discussion I had with a manager who rang me one day and said, 'Look, I don't know whether you remember me, but I was on one of your courses about two years ago. I was wondering if you could advise me on a good course which would help me learn something about motivation.'

As it happened, I did remember this person and the job he had held in his organization. He seemed fairly clear in his own mind that he wanted a specific solution – a course he could go on. Initially I accepted this diagnosis. We started talking about possible courses.

'How long would you like the course to last?'

'Oh, about two days to a week. I couldn't take any longer off at this stage.'

'What is it you would particularly like to obtain from the course?'

'Mainly, how to bring people together and motivate them, to get changes introduced.'

I then put forward a general proposal to test the water. 'When we last met, the course you were on was fairly specialized. I think that in your new role you need more of a general management course.'

Problems before solutions

His reply indicated that this solution-centred approach was not relevant to his problem. 'I don't want to go over the whole field of marketing, industrial relations, production,' he said. 'My particular concern is how to get this department working.'

At last the alarm bells began to ring. Here I was accepting the assumption that he needed yet another course. I was going down the same path, rather than questioning his assumption. I was starting with a solution rather than trying to work out what the problem was. This is a common error that we all make, particularly if the client seems confident in what he is saying, and gives the impression of having thought about the situation.

I therefore changed direction. 'How will the course relate to your job?'

'Well, that's interesting. Since we last met I've been promoted. You see I am in a difficult position because I have to try to bring two departments together, but the existing bosses of those departments do not retire until later in the year. I have been working for the last four months with both of these departments, which have recently been merged into one, so as to get some experience of what they actually do. However, it is extremely frustrating, as no one will listen to me while the existing two bosses are there, and they certainly won't cooperate with each other.'

Suddenly the conversation had moved from a solution-based discussion of 'What course can I go on?' to the real personalities and politics involved.

Personal meetings important

I also sensed in the discussion that my contact, who had not seen me for two years, was a bit hesitant about talking in detail over the telephone. I therefore said that in order to talk the matter over properly we might need more time, and it would be best if we could meet for lunch. He didn't immediately respond to this, but talked a little more about the problems he was facing. After a few minutes he said he thought it might be useful to have lunch and we agreed upon a date.

Over lunch, he told me in considerable detail the problems he was having as a manager. Up until six months ago he had been involved solely in technical work. He was asked to move, at short notice, to a new department and become the assistant manager, after which he would become the head of the department when the existing manager retired. Shortly afterwards, this department (department A) was merged with another department (department B). The head of department B was also retiring in about four months' time and my friend was told that he would then become the senior manager in charge of integrating these two departments. In the intervening time he had to learn what these departments did, and develop a strategy for integrating them.

Right from the beginning he found difficulty. In section A there was suspicion of him. In section B there was a deliberate attempt to obstruct him, in that people would not give him information, accede to requests, or comply with his instructions. Because he had not formally taken over, he felt that he was in a limbo situation and could not set the pace he wanted.

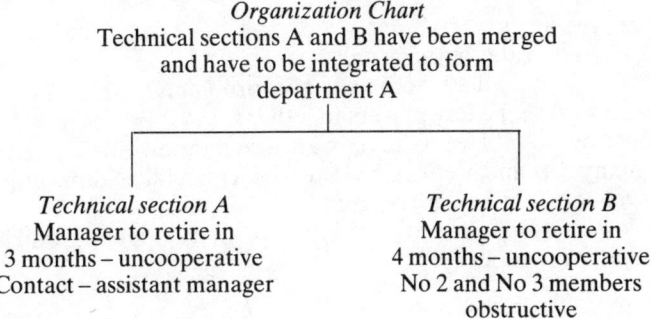

Organization Chart
Technical sections A and B have been merged
and have to be integrated to form
department A

Technical section A	*Technical section B*
Manager to retire in	Manager to retire in
3 months – uncooperative	4 months – uncooperative
Contact – assistant manager	No 2 and No 3 members
	obstructive

The need to manage the politics

Here is a classic example of the theatre of consulting. There is a central actor (the contact client) surrounded by other actors, all with their scripts and the plot which was hatched long before the client arrived. But can he change the play? If he cannot, then he will probably not survive. He needs to rewrite the main script, change the roles, alter the plot and try to get a happy ending. But it is not easy. Much managerial consultation therefore involves a careful reading of the theatre of management and skilled coaching on the redirection of effort.

What would you do as a consultant? I decided that process consultation was the best initial approach. I asked a number of open-ended questions. He indicated the situation was very difficult and was negative. I made him confront these feelings and consider positive things he could do. This involved thinking through who he wanted reporting to him and the structure he wanted. He agreed to go back and let people know what he required and to involve people so he could see who was on whose side. He left the meeting saying he had found it valuable to meet and was now clear what he was going to do and how he was going to do it.

Guidelines

In consultative assignments you have to identify the actors, their roles, their scripts and how to manage them to get things done. One of the most important things is to get people who do not normally meet, but need to in order to resolve business problems, to do so. This is a crucial task.

In doing so you can help them ensure their script is related to the relevant tasks and people are fulfilling the correct roles. This is a most important job as otherwise people will not use their talents to the full. Consequently the work of the organization will be done ineffectively and inefficiently. Your role in the theatre of organizational life is to ensure the play is a success and people can be involved with the necessary permission to enter the appropriate territory.

Some questions you can ask to guide your thoughts are:

- Who are the key players?
- What are their roles in the drama?
- To what extent do they meet to resolve problems?
- How can I bring the key players together?
- What scripts should we write to overcome natural and planned plots?
- How many acts and scenes do we need or can it all be done quickly?
- What rehearsal, if any, is required?
- How do we ensure the audience knows what is happening and how they should actively support?

16 Factors influencing failure and success

'Myself when young did eagerly frequent
Doctor and Saint, and heard great Argument
About it and about: but evermore
Came out by the same Door as in I Went'

The Rubaiyat of Omar Khayyám, transl. Edward Fitzgerald

Managing consultative processes

People who are successful at consulting are invariably effective at the process level. This means they are able to establish the appropriate ways and means of getting people to solve problems and opportunities. They create an environment where people can talk positively and get action. A number of the processes they introduce are simple and straightforward in retrospect but not always at the time. I have illustrated some examples in this book from my own experience such as

- getting pilots together to talk about managing an aircrew
- getting supervisors, administrators, sales people and technical people together to discuss reducing costs
- getting area bank managers together to discuss the development of the branch managers
- getting most managers together to visit each other's stores.

All of the above may sound rather obvious things to do if you want to improve people's performance. However, in each and every case these people had not previously met to resolve such issues. There was no process available for them to do so. It had to be created.

Now this approach to consulting is rather different from the model where someone comes in and does an investigation and provides you with a report advising you what to do.

The approach I now use wherever possible is to get the managers themselves to conduct the investigation. In that way they can learn for themselves what is right and what is wrong. My role is to guide and advise on the processes and methods. In this way managers learn to consult for themselves. If it is appropriate, I will contribute to that process with a report but the final submissions should be with those who 'own' the problem or opportunity.

179

The strategic consulting choices

There are, as I see it, two models, which I shall refer to as 1 and 2, which you can use.

Strategy 1
1   Client presents problem/opportunity challenge.
2   Consultant gathers data from nominated people.
3   Consultant writes a report.
4   Report sent to client and discussed.
5   Findings and action agreed and participants notified what to do.

Strategy 2
1   Client identifies problem/opportunity.
2   Consultant and client agree who should meet.
3   Consultant facilitates meeting(s) where key people define needs.
4   Consultant agrees with these participants to feed back and how it should be made.
5   Consultant and client meet participants for feedback to determine action and how it should be progressed.

Key concepts of use

In using Strategy 2, I have found a number of concepts of great importance and I have summarized them here as a basis for note.

Experience: This is the greatest asset that people in organizations have and often it is not used. An effective consultant will be able to tap into the collective experiences of the members and bring them together to improve things.

Energy: I look closely for who has got energy to tackle the issues. That is where you must put your effort. Otherwise you will dissipate your efforts and get lost. If you are not talking to people who have the energy to do something, then reallocate your time and find those people who do have the required drive.

Determination: On any assignment things rarely run smoothly. You can assume that the normal curve of a typical assignment will look as follows:

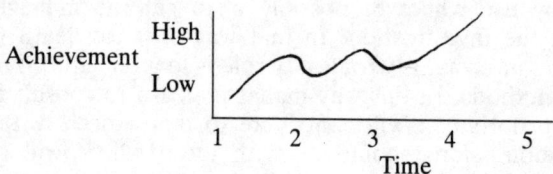

The curve will go up and down and often plateau. You must continue with determination, knowing that if you are using the appropriate processes you will gradually move up the curve.

Interview checklist for consultants

A valuable checklist to guide discussion is provided by Goodge (1987) and the following questions have been adapted from his proposals which were originally constructed for use in organizing an assessment centre. How effective are you when in the consulting role, based on these points?

1 *Relationship* Helping client to relax.   Y/N
2 *Purpose* Agreed the purpose of the meeting.   Y/N
3 *Information Seeking* Sought important information he or she did not have (eg client's views, vital facts).   Y/N
4 *Understanding* Tested his or her understanding regularly.   Y/N
5 *Information Giving* Clearly conveyed information the client needed   Y/N
6 *Client Proposals* Invited the client to propose a solution.   Y/N
7 *Development* Built upon the client's ideas where possible.   Y/N
8 *Consultant* Provided ideas and suggestions when the meeting became stuck.   Y/N
9 *Process* Ensured that the meeting stayed on course.   Y/N
10 *Action* Agreed a detailed plan of action.   Y/N
11 *Summary* Summarized the agreements reached.   Y/N

Based on my own experience I believe that if you are able to manage these eleven processes well you will more often than not be successful in your consulting assignments.

Discipline: I don't subscribe to a bureaucratic approach, but I do support a strong discipline. This involves setting output dates, establishing roles, clarifying who does what and when and working hard to keep to the plan. The discipline of doing things regularly and often is the secret of progress.

Expectations: People often get what they expect. It is your job to set high expectations both of what people should contribute and what they can gain. Let people know in advance what is required and, if it is going to be hard, say so. Then people are conditioned and can decide whether to be in or out. If you want people to support an initiative, you have in the best sense to condition them by setting high expectations.

Follow up: Too many assignments fall down because there is a lack of attention to follow up. Again the follow up must be systematic rather than *ad hoc*. Dates need to be put in diaries and people asked to report on what they have done and what they will do next.

Atmosphere: Your job as a consultant should help create the atmosphere in which people will do their best. If the atmosphere is 'wrong' then stop the assignment and get people round a table to discuss their feelings. It is best to clear the air, then you can get on with the job.

Reinforce success: Very often consultant advisers are seen as people who find weaknesses. That is right and proper if there are areas that need improving. Equally there can be a number of good things happening in an organization. Your job is to reinforce and build on these. This is particularly so when you see good things happening on your assignment. Say so, and let people know. In that way, success will breed success.

In all consulting situations there are particular issues which can influence success. These issues may change in emphasis from one project to another. However, there are a number of important areas of our work that recur and need to be considered if we are to gain regular success. We shall examine some of these issues.

Useful consultative feedback

Consultant advisers are renowned for writing reports, perhaps more than for any other skill of the profession. However, I do question how many of these reports are read and understood. Even if they are read and understood, I wonder how far people take action upon the ideas and recommendations. Therefore a central issue in the success of any assignment is how you feed back reliable and valid information to clients in order to get action.

In many organizations I have been to they tell me of the consultants they have had previously. They say consultants have sent them a fat report, collected their fee and nothing has changed. Of course we can question also who is to blame for this situation. Clearly the clients have not received what they actually wanted, although the consultants may well feel they have done their job.

I learnt this lesson very early in my own consultant advisory work when I was asked to work with a textile organization which was concerned with the market for its products. Although the central task involved the marketing of their product, there were also motivational issues, as the staff felt the organization was not performing well.

I started by gathering a mass of information. I looked at the facts and figures of the organization's performance and also gathered facts and figures on the market and the opportunities. I had the opportunity to talk with key staff members and gather their perceptions and views. Eventually I submitted to the managing director what I thought was a comprehensive report. It recorded the situation as I saw it. I had certainly put a lot of work into it and felt that I had done justice to the assignment.

I than had a telephone call from the managing director to say that he would like a meeting with me and the chairman of the company. I could see from the way they started the discussion that they were not enthusiastic about the report. The chairman summed it up by saying, 'This is a very long report, but what exactly does it mean?' We continued to discuss the issues for a while but at the end of the meeting I could see that they felt the document had not really met their needs.

Why was it that I had put in so much work and yet when we came to the final presentation things had not gone as well as I or the client had anticipated? Clearly I had missed the point. The report, although based upon solid research and citing numerous facts and figures, was not sufficient.

Listen to the key people

It seems obvious now that I had missed several of the most important points. First of all I had not interviewed either the managing director or the chairman, although they were critical people in the system. I had not taken the time to sit down with them and gather their views and include them in the report. I had taken the brief as given and assumed that they wanted me to talk to other people.

If I had started with them and gathered their views it is probable that when the report was represented they would have taken a greater interest in the conclusions insofar as it reflected their inputs. It is important to obtain the commitment of senior managers from the beginning to ensure that projects started will be followed through.

Feed back draft comments

Secondly, I had not taken the trouble to feed back the early draft of my report to the people with whom I had talked in the organization. I had not been able to verify what I had written prior to the final submission. I have now learnt from practical experience that even if you cannot get those people together you should send a draft report to them so that they can write back and make comments on it before the final version is submitted.

Reflect the concerns as well as the facts

Thirdly, I had concentrated too much on the facts and figures. I had not represented particular concerns of the people with whom I had talked. The importance of recording and feeding back verbatim the points of view of key people is something which is essential if you wish to develop a genuine problem solving discussion in an organization.

Provide opportunities for problem solving

Fourthly, I had written a report but not developed a consulting plan to enable the clients to problem-solve the issues. I had assumed that they would take this report to their normal executive meetings and it would then be dealt with in the normal way. However, I should have realized that one of my roles as a consultant adviser was perhaps to call people together in combinations which would not normally meet, in order to break down organizational barriers relating to the problem. Perhaps I was the one who could get the chairman, MD and people four levels down to talk together in a way that had never been done before. All I had to do was invite them – but I didn't.

Reports as a process not as a solution

In short, a report is not enough. It is no wonder that so many consultants never really produce change. I learnt this early lesson and subsequently took a very different attitude to providing clients with feedback. In essence, the report is no longer the greater part of the consulting process. It is a vehicle to facilitate the process of discussion amongst people in the organization who must ultimately solve the problems.

Therefore I believe the report should be the result of what people are concerned about and their views on actions that could be taken. The report then becomes the basis for facilitating discussions with these people on how to improve things. Instead of the report being seen as a product it becomes part of the process of problem solving.

The consulting process

Too many consultants have seen the delivery of a report as the central aspect of their task. I believe this is to take rather an objective and detached view of consulting. Instead I see the report merely as part of the subjective process of getting people to exchange their views and reach agreements on how to improve activity within an organization.

Fritz Steele (1975), who has written widely on his experiences as a consultant, said, 'Most people spend their professional energy fixing events, not on improving the patterns of action.' Therefore he advocated we should for the most part focus on the ways clients are tackling problems rather than providing *ad hoc* solutions. Ultimately clients must be able to move on independent of consultation. That is a measure of the consultant's success.

To achieve this Steele suggests consultants should organize meetings that:

- keep to time
- identify purposes
- agree agendas
- outline process – brainstorming, reporting, etc.
- establish decision processes
- monitor relevance – long speeches or low contributions

- visibly record points
- keep the pace up
- ask for next steps
- critique and review.

These accord with my experience and provide a useful basis for managing an advisory assignment. Ultimately the client must take responsibility for the action and implementation and that is the decisive test.

Some keys to success and failure in consulting assignments

Failure can be caused by:

1 Not involving influential persons early enough – the make or break people.
2 Proposing solutions before problems are diagnosed.
3 Presenting reports full of content without an equal regard for the process of discussion.
4 Moving too quickly, causing surprises and creating defensive behaviour amongst clients.
5 Not recognizing the effect of change in one part of the system on another part of the system.

Success is usually dependent upon:

1 Spending time in understanding the cues and clues.
2 Accurate summaries of issues raised and effective conversational control.
3 In-depth contracting and agreement to ensure an action is on a solid base.
4 Attention to the political processes of the client's organization and the involvement of the relevant people.
5 Delivery on time to the required standard.
6 The management of the assignment by establishing a structure through which all involved can resolve issues.

How clients see you

I have had the opportunity to work with a number of consultants and advisers and to watch how they relate with their clients. In some cases I have been the client myself. In other situations I have been working on a joint venture. It has always interested me to see how colleagues engaged in consultancy advisory work relate to their clients. The way clients see you determines whether they are prepared to 'open doors' for you and continue your involvement.

Energy

The energy level of others depends on the energy level that you personally put into the assignment. You do not need to be super active. You do need, however, to show a high level of interest. Your presentation and projection are vital aspects of your approach. We all radiate certain messages to our clients and we can be aware of and control these.

What do you deliver?

Clients will judge you on substance, not just style. This means you have to deliver. Your performance must match your promise. They will continue looking to see if you appear on time, meet programme deadlines, keep to costs, honour agreements, meet quality standards and a host of other important points. You are judged on outputs, not just inputs. As an old consultant said, 'It's not just doing it right that counts, but getting it right.' Remember outputs each and every day are what clients want. If you don't know what they are, start asking questions quickly.

Understanding others

For example, in a recent discussion, one of my clients said, 'When I first joined this organization I was told there was a morale problem. I have heard that said many times over the years. Now I am being told again that there is a morale problem. I don't believe it's any worse now than it was when I first joined.'

I had spent some time in the organization with various groups of people. The majority of people I met said that there was a morale problem and gave evidence to support it. The question is, at this point should I radiate to the client that I disagree with him or seek to understand his particular point of view? I chose the latter and asked him to expand more on his view of the situation and why other people felt that there was such a problem.

He agreed that if people perceived that there was such a problem, it should be tackled, otherwise it could become a self-fulfilling prophecy. It was on this basis that we moved forward. Rather than radiating to him that I doubted his judgement, I radiated that I was trying to understand his position *vis-à-vis* what other people were saying, and looking for a problem solving way of tackling different perceptions.

What do you radiate?

We radiate what we are thinking by the way we behave. A lot has been said about non verbal behaviour. Clearly, if you have your arms folded, your legs crossed, your body slanted away from the client and your head tossed back in the air looking at the ceiling, this will give some indication of what you are radiating to a client. Equally, if you are leaning forward with your arms on the table, hands open, eyes fixed on what the client is saying, and giving an indication that you are open and interested, then this will also radiate your approach. It is important to convey your involvement in a non verbal way, just as it is important to do so through your conversation.

It is not always in the words that you use, but the tone of voice and mannerisms, and even in the way in which you dress. What we radiate to our clients is critical to success. For example, it is possible to radiate confidence, trust, experience, understanding, and various other factors that will positively affect the project. Equally, I have seen the clients generate anxiety, doubt, superiority, impatience, and disinterest, all of which have had an ill effect upon the project.

When you meet with clients what are you trying to radiate? In my own case, I would say first of all I try to radiate genuine concern and understanding of what it is that the client is saying. My initial aim is to convince the client that I really want to hear what he or she has to say and take their views and opinions seriously, whether or not they are correct. That does not mean to say that I agree with them, but I should radiate that I understand them.

Clients are usually sensitive to what you are radiating. It is no use trying to radiate something that you are not. If you are doubtful, then this will come through, so why not be open about it with your clients? If you are under pressure, this will also in most cases radiate itself from you to your client. The same will be true if you're nervous or overconfident.

Self understanding

This is one of the reasons why I believe it is so important that you learn to understand yourself and build upon your strengths. Just as a golfer can look at a videotape of his or her performance, so it is important for you to get some personal feedback on how you come across to others. This perhaps can be done through joint venture assignments where you can talk over with your client how you are seen by others. However, perhaps the best source of feedback is to ask a trusted client. If they have been working with you for a while, they will know your own strengths and weaknesses. Of course, they may be biased comments because they appreciate your approach sufficiently to retain you. Therefore, from time to time, it is useful to find out from people who you find it difficult to work with what you radiate and how they respond.

Raising energy levels and what we radiate to our clients are two crucial elements of the consulting advisory role. I have seen many technically competent consultant advisers who could not raise other people's energy levels because they could not radiate the right behavioural message. Either they could not 'read the situation' or they could not adapt their behaviour.

Consulting Example
Characteristics required by consultants

There are few books written directly by consultants for consultants. An exception is that by Greiner and Metzger entitled *Consulting to Management*. They reflect on what makes an effective consultant and draw the following profile.

Diagnostic ability: with the attributes of being objective, curiosity, conceptual and analytical ability and the capability of inductive reasoning, taking every situation as new.

Solution skills: where the consultant helps create the answers through imagination, the courage to propose change and the ability to teach and guide the client.

Knowledge: in many different forms where the consultant is aware of the theory and research and applied techniques.

Communication skills: where the consultant has top listening skills combined with exceptional ability to feed back accurate data in writing and in representations, while making effective interventions in the real time meetings.

Marketing and selling: where the stragegy adopted is consonant with the values of the process of consulting.

Managerial ability: where the consultant can manage him or herself and also lead a project team to achieve targets to deadlines within a budget.

Personality characteristics: are regarded as key factors, as clients ultimately buy the professional services of the consultant as a person. This involves a personality that can be flexible to move from assignment to assignment and bring to each positive thinking, high ethics, energy and other personal attributes.

These are some of the factors that clients look for in consultants and they provide a useful checklist for us to measure ourselves against.

How to avoid failure

Projects can succeed or fail for a variety of reasons. However, it is usually true to say that while you need lots of things to go right to ensure success you only need one or two things to go wrong to bring about failure.

The following points can therefore be useful:

Client clarification of contract

Spend as much time as you can finding out what the client really wants, when and how. Don't take a bald statement as a brief. Keep close to the client as you proceed in case their definition of the requirement changes.

Gather relevant data

Listen for the cues and clues. Don't be seduced by content. Question why things don't work. Get people to talk in groups rather than just individually. In this way you might find out what is relevant.

Easy data feedback

Make sure your presentation of data is in line with the way clients can most easily understand your feedback. The report requires hard individual reading effort by the client. If you feel your client will not take easily to this, then help ensure the presentation is done in a different way through personal meetings, the use of visual aids and any medium that will facilitate problem-solving.

Communicate to strengths

The process of communication is as important as the content. Study whether your client likes data in a numeric, verbal, visual and/or numeric form, then try to orientate the information to his or her strength.

Implications analysis

Look for system effects of your advice. Consider the impact of your proposals in terms of the organizational arrangements and assess if improvement in one area will have a negative impact on other areas. If so, be proactive and do something about it.

Positive news

Clients, like most of us, don't like nasty surprises. Provide your news in a positive way. Talk of improvements rather than inadequacies. Get people to emphasize what can be done. Discuss problems from the basis of an opportunity to improve. Don't depress the client.

Respect the culture

As a consultant adviser you work on other people's territory. You need to be aware of their culture and respect particular traditions. Therefore, be flexible when it is necessary, without using the problems created as an excuse for not completing the task. From time to time you may be asked to help change the culture. Start by understanding and respecting the existing culture.

Grapevines for discovery

Use the grapevine of informal meetings. People often will communicate more freely when not on work territory. Provide opportunities for people to talk to you informally.

Political involvement

Find out who can make or break your project because of their strong political connections. Involve them early in the consultation and diagnosis. Seek to have them involved as advisers on a regular basis.

The basis for successful consulting

Success depends on a little luck and a lot of hard work, particularly persistence. It was Calvin Coolidge who said, 'Nothing in this world can take the place of persistence. Talent will not; nothing is more common than unsuccessful men with great talent. Genius will not; unrewarded genius is almost a proverb. Education will not; the world is full of educated derelicts. Persistence, determination alone are omnipotent.'

Einstein supported this proposition when he said his achievements were one per cent inspiration and ninety-nine per cent perspiration. So work at it, but work to a system.

We are all consultants at various times in our lives. We all have our own style and approach. That is the way it should be. The principles in this book should be adapted to your own natural way of assisting others to learn, change and improve.

There is no easy route to success in consulting as in any other aspect of work. However, we can all improve our managerial consulting by considering the principles as identified, based on the experience and the cases in this book.

In summary I see that we all have to be effective at what I shall call the seven Ds of consulting.

1   *Define* what you are being asked to do carefully by asking the client(s) what they want to achieve as an output.

2 *Diagnose* what or who is getting in the way by doing some investigations. Remember to bring people together who don't normally meet together to discuss issues face to face.

3 *Design* in conjunction with your client something that will be an improvement on the present approach.

4 *Develop* a means of implementing the design so it becomes operational.

5 *Deliver* the new approach so everyone knows what to do, by training people and giving them both the tools and knowledge to change.

6 *Delegate* to the client the involvement and implementation at all levels. Remember your task is to be the consultant adviser, not take over the manager's job.

7 *Debrief* through debate and discussion on a regular structured basis what has been learnt and what can be done next.

These simple steps form the essence of effective managerial consulting and provide a sound basis for practice.

Finally I shall finish as I began, with some consulting advice from William Shakespeare, who as so often sums up the key points so succinctly. He suggested, in *Hamlet*:

> 'Give every man thine ear, but few thy voice;
> Take each man's censure, but reserve
> thy judgement . . . .
> This above all: to thine own self be true,
> And it must follow, as the night the day,
> Thou canst not then be false to any man.'

Guidelines

The above processes are integral to the three action areas which must govern all consulting as outlined below.

Action planning

Planning is a vital element in any change process. It is often seen as a detailed logical process done in advance. However, that is rarely so. There can be an initial blueprint as with an architect's drawing, but thereafter the plan needs to evolve depending on the requirements of the situation.

One aspect of the plan, however, can and should remain firm and that relates to the mission and values you, the client and the organization establish and work towards. Frequently organization change goes wrong because the fundamental purpose of the people and their efforts have not been clearly worked out.

Beyond that I see planning as an ongoing activity where those who need to be committed to the decision are involved. It requires skills in bringing people together to create visions before you start working out the detail and the numbers. This can be done in creative workshops or brainstorming meetings.

Action research

The consulting processes are primarily based upon helping people plan, find out what they need and facilitating improved action. It sounds simple and straightforward. In reality it isn't because things and people get in the way. Therefore understanding the processes of finding out is essential to complement the technical knowledge and skill you have.

Action implementation

This should be an extension of action research and action planning rather than something separate. It is the focus how, rather than what or why. It is the process where tangible outputs have to emerge against cost and time deadlines.

Exercise

1   What are the three main things you can do in the next three months to improve your managerial consulting skills?

2   What is your plan for improvement?

3   How will you measure your improvement?

References

Argyris, C., 'Explorations in Consulting Client Relationships', *Human Organization*, vol. 20, 1961.

Argyris, C., *Intervention Theory and Method*, Addison-Wesley, 1970.

Argyris, C., *Action Science*, Jossey Bass, 1985.

Beckhard, R., 'The Confrontation Meeting', *Harvard Business Review*, vol. 45, 1967.

Beckhard, R., *Organization Development*, Addison-Wesley, 1969.

Beckhard, R. and Harris R., *Organizational Transitions: Managing Complex Change*, Addison-Wesley, 1977.

Bell, C. and Nadler, L., *The Client Consultant Handbook*, Gulf Publishing, 1979.

Bennett, R., 'Auditing Performance – an alternative approach', *Leadership and Organization Development Journal*, vol. 3 (1), 1982.

Bennis, R., *Organization Development*, Addison-Wesley, 1969.

Bennis, W., *Changing Organizations*, McGraw-Hill, 1966.

Bennis, W. G., 'Theory and Method in Applying Behavioural Science to Planned Organization Change', A Bertlett and T. Kayser, *Changing Organizations Behaviour*, Prentice-Hall, 1973.

Bennis, W., Benne, K., Chin R. and Corey, K., *The Planning of Change*, Holt, Rinehart & Winston, 1976.

Blake R. and Mouton, R. S., *Consultation*, Addison-Wesley, 1976.

Block, P., *A Guide To Flawless Consulting*, University Associates, 1981.

Carkhuff, R., *Helping and Human Relations*, Holt, Rinehart & Winston, 1969.

Casey, D., 'A Diagnostic Model for the O.D. Consultant', *Journal of European Industrial Training*, vol. 4 (1), 1975.

Casey, D., 'Some Processes at the Consultant/Client Interface in O.D. Work', *Leadership and Organization Development Journal*, vol. 3 (1), 1982.

Davey, N. G., 'The Consultants Role in Organizational Change', *MSU Business Topics*, vol. 19 (2), 1971.

Drucker, P., *The Effective Executive*, Pan, 1967.

Drucker, P., *The Adventures of a Bystander*, Heinemann, 1982.

Edmonstone, J., 'The Realities of Organizational Consultancy', *Leadership and Organizational Development Journal*, vol. 1 (2), 1980.

Egan, G., *The Skilled Helper*, Brooks/Cole, 1975.

Ferguson, C., 'Concerning the Nature of Human Systems and the Consultants Role', *Journal of Applied Behavioural Science*, (4), April/June 1968.

Frankel, V., *Psychotherapy and Existentialism*, Penguin Books, 1973.

French, W. and Bell, C., *Organization Development*, Prentice-Hall, 1978.

Friedlander, F., 'A Comparative Study of Consulting Processes and Group Development', *Journal of Applied Behavioural Science*, vol. 1, (4), 1968.

Fuchs, J., *Making the Most of Management Consulting Services*, Amacom, 1985.

Ganesh, S., 'Organization Consultants – A comparison of styles', *Human Relations*, vol. 31 (1), 1978.

Geneen, H. and Moscow, D., *Managing*, Doubleday, 1984.

Goldhamer, H., *The Adviser*, Elsevier, North Holland, 1978.

Goodge, P., 'Assessment Centres: Time for Deregulation', *Management Education and Development*, vol. 18, Pt 2, 1987.

Goodstein, L., *Consulting with Human Service Systems*, Addison-Wesley, 1978.

Gouldner, A., 'Explorations in Applied Social Science', *Social Problems* 3, 1956.

Greiner, L., 'Patterns of Organization Change', *Harvard Business Review*, May/June 1967.

Greiner L. and Metzger, R., *Consulting to Management*, Prentice-Hall, 1983.

Handy, C., *Gods to Management: How they work and why they will fail*, Pan Books, London/Sydney, 1979.

Harrison, R., 'Choosing the Depth of an Organizational Intervention', *Journal of Applied Behavioural Science*, no. 6, 1970.

Hunt, A., *The Management Consultant*, Ronald Press, 1977.

Jacques, E., *The Changing Culture of the Factory*, Tavistock, 1951.

Kelley, R., 'Should You Have an Internal Consultant?' *Harvard Business Review*, vol. 57 (6), 1979.

Kellogg, D., 'Contrasting Successful and Unsuccessful O.D. Consultation Relationships', *Group and Organization Studies*, vol. 9 (2), 1984.

Kubr, M. (ed.), *Management Consulting: A guide to the profession*, International Labour Office, Geneva, 1987.

Kakabadse, A., *Organizational Politics*, Gower, 1984.

Kakabadse, A., 'The Consultant's Role', *Journal of Managerial Psychology*, vol. 1 (2), 1987.

Kakabadse, A., 'How to Use Consultants', *International Journal of Manpower*, vol. 4 (1), 1988.

Klein, L., *A Social Scientist in Industry*, Gower, 1976.

Kolb, D. and Frohman, A., 'An OD Approach to Consulting', *Sloan Management Review*, vol. 12, (1), 1970.

Lawrence P. and Lorsch, J., *Developing Organizations: Diagnosis and Action,* Addison-Wesley, 1969.

Leavitt, H., 'Applied Organization Change in Industry', Chapter 27 in *Handbook of Organizations,* J. March (ed.), Rand McNally, 1965.

Lewin, K., *Field Theory in Social Science,* Associated Publishers, 1963.

Likert, R., *New Patterns of Management,* McGraw-Hill, 1961.

Likert, R., *The Human Organization,* McGraw-Hill, 1967.

Lippitt, G., *Organization Renewal,* Appleton Century Crofts, 1971.

Lippitt, G., *Visualizing Change,* University Associates, 1973.

Lippitt, G. (ed.), 'The Role of the Training Director as an Internal Consultant', *Journal of European Industrial Training,* vol. 4 (5), 1975.

Lippitt, G., 'A Study of the Consultation Process', *Journal of Social Issues,* vol. 15 (2), 1960.

Lippitt, G. and Lippitt, R., *The Consulting Process in Action,* University Associates, 1978.

Lippitt, R., Watson, J. and Westley, B., *The Dynamics of Planned Change,* Harcourt Brace, 1958.

Mangham, I., *The Politics of Organizational Change,* Associated Business Press, 1979.

Margerison, C. J., *Influencing Organizational Change,* Institute of Personnel Management, London 1978.

Margerison, C. J., 'The Adviser's Role in Organizational Change' in *Psychology at Work,* P. Warr (ed.), Penguin, 1980.

Margerison, C. J., 'How to Avoid Failure and Gain Success in Management Development', *Journal of Management Development,* vol. 1, (3), 1982.

Margerison, C. J., *Conversation Control Skills for Managers,* W. H. Allen, 1987a.

Margerison, C. J., *How to Improve Your Managerial Performance,* MCB University Press, 1987b.

Margerison, C. J., 'Existential Management Development' in *Management Development,* C. Cox and J. Beck (eds), Wiley, 1984.

Margerison, C. J., Davies, R. and McCann, D., 'High Flying Management Development', *Training & Development Journal,* February 1987.

Margerison, C. J. and McCann, D., *How to Lead a Winning Team,* MCB University Press, 1984a.

Margerison, C. J. and McCann, D., *The Team Management Index,* MCB University Press, 1984b.

Margerison, C. J. and Roden, S., *Management Development Bibliography,* MCB University Press, 1987.

Marguilies, N. and Raia, R., *Conceptual Foundations of Organization Development,* McGraw-Hill, 1978.

Marguilies, N. and Wallace, J., *Organizational Change: Techniques and Applications,* Scott, Foresman & Coy, 1973.

Menzel, R., 'A Taxonomy of Change-Agent Skills', *Journal of European Training,* vol. 4 (5), 1975.

Miner, J., 'The Management Consultant First as a Source of High Level Managerial Talent', *Academy of Management Journal,* vol. 16 (2), 1973.

Morris, J. and Burgoyne, J., *Developing Resourceful Managers*, Institute of Personnel Management, 1975.

Nadler, D., *Feedback and Organization Development*, Addison-Wesley, 1977.

Peters T. and Waterman, R., *In Search of Excellence*, Harper & Row, 1982.

Peters T. and Waterman, R., 'Structure is not Organization', *Business Horizons*, 1980.

Reason, P. and Rowan, J., *Human Inquiry*, J. Wiley, 1981.

Reddin, W. J., *Confessions of an Organizational Change Agent: Group and Organizational Studies*, March 1977.

Revans, R., *Developing Effective Managers*, Praeger, 1971.

Revans, R., *The Origins and Growth of Action Learning*, Chartwell Bratt, 1982.

Rogers, C., *Client Centred Therapy*, Houghton Mifflin, 1951.

Rogers, C., 'The Characteristics of a Helping Relationship', *Personnel and Guidance Journal*, vol. 37 (1), 1958.

Rowbottom, R., *Social Analysis*, Heinemann, 1977.

Schein, E., *Process Consultation*, Addison-Wesley, 1969.

Schmidt, W. and Johnson, A., 'A Continuum of Consultancy Styles', in Edgar F. Huse, *Organization Development and Change*, West Publishing Co, 1975.

Sinha, D., *Consultants and Consulting Styles*, Vision Books, 1979.

Skinner, B. F., *Beyond Freedom and Dignity*, Bantam, 1971.

Steele, F., *Consulting for Organizational Change*, University of Massachusetts Press, 1975.

Steele, F., *The Role of the Internal Consultant*, CBI Publishing Co, 1982.

Steele, F., 'Consultants and Detectives', *Journal of Applied Behavioural Science*, vol. 5 (2), 1969.

Strauss, A. and Bavelas, A., The Hovey Beard Case.

Tichy, N., 'Agents of Planned Change', *Administrative Science Quarterly*, vol. 19 (2), 1974.

Tilles, S., 'Understanding the Consultant's Role', *Harvard Business Review*, vol. 39, (6), 1961.

Tisdall, P., *Agents for Change*, Heinemann, 1982.

Trist, E., et al *Organizational Choice*, Tavistock, 1963.

Walton, R., *Interpersonal Peacemaking*, Addison-Wesley, 1969.

Waterman, R., Peters, T. and Philips, J., 'Structure is Not Organization', *Business Horizons*, June 1980.

Wills, G. and Day, A., 'Buckingham's New Action Learning Business School', *Journal of European Industrial Training*, vol. 8 (6), 1984.

Woodworth, W. and Reed, N., 'Witch Doctors, Messianics, Sorcerers and O.D. Consultants: parallels and paradigms', *Organizational Dynamics*, Autumn 1979.

Zaltman, G. and Duncan, R., *Strategies for Planned Change*, Wiley, 1977.

Index